D1744234

Walk!

the

Isle of Wight

with

Martin Simons

DISCOVERY WALKING GUIDES LTD

Walk! Isle of Wight
First Edition - May 2007
Copyright © 2007

Published by
Discovery Walking Guides Ltd
10 Tennyson Close, Northampton NN5 7HJ,
England

Mapping supplied by **Global Mapping Limited**
(www.globalmapping.com)

Mapping sourced from | Ordnance Survey® This product includes mapping data licensed from **Ordnance Survey®** with the permission of the Controller of Her Majesty's Stationery Office. © Crown Copyright 2005. All rights reserved.

Licence Number 40044851

Photographs
All photographs in this book were taken by the author.

Front Cover Photographs

Walk 2   Walk 1

Walk 6   Walk 19

ISBN 978904946342
ASIB 1-904946-34-8

Text and photographs © Martin Simons

All rights reserved. No part of this publication may be reproduced, stored in a retrieval system or transmitted in any form or by any means, electronic, mechanical, photocopying, recording or otherwise, without the prior written permission of the publishers.

The authors and publishers have tried to ensure that the information and maps in this publication are as accurate as possible. However, we accept no responsibility for any loss, injury or inconvenience sustained by anyone using this book.

Walk!
The Isle of Wight

CONTENTS

THE WALKS

THE AUTHOR

Martin Simons is a retired Civil Engineer. He was born in Bromley, Kent, and raised in South East London, where a 360 acre park 'playground', literally over the back fence, nurtured an affinity with nature in the suburbs.

Martin moved to the Sussex Coast, where he lives, near both beach and Downs, with his wife, Gilly. Their four children have fled the nest, two internationally to Mexico and Tenerife, one to London, as a TV presenter, and one locally. Martin's treasured first grandchild, Tonito, lives in Mexico, the second, Zachary (with a sibling 'bump' on the way), is born and bred in Sussex!

For many years, Martin was involved in girls' and women's football, managing cup and championship winning teams with Brighton and Hove Albion.

Walking the South Downs and the Isle of Wight succeeded football as a dominant leisure activity, which soon matured into a passion – and then a mission! Existing walking guides consistently failed to impress, and were judged to be lacking in both accuracy and imagination. Martin was soon poring over OS Explorer maps, meticulously planning and recording the very best walking routes on the Island. This book is the culmination of his endeavours.

Martin Simons is also the author of:

Walk! The South Downs
ISBN 9781904946144 (1-904946-14-3)
published by Discovery Walking Guides Ltd.

Acknowledgements

My wife, Gilly, for her continuing encouragement and support, Dave Sargent for keeping me company on some of the walks, and Jo Hind for her excellent editorial advice, which has proved invaluable. I am indebted to Helen Martin of Stagecoach buses, Kerry Jackson of Wightlink, and Marc Morgan-Huws of Southern Vectis for their travel sponsorship. And finally, thanks to David and Ros Brawn for putting together my second book.

INTRODUCTION

From the moment you step on the ferry, the adventure begins! I can recall the wonder of my first visit to the Island as a child, and even though I have returned countless times since, that sense of excitement persists to this day.

The Isle of Wight is different, almost a step back in time, with a slower pace and more relaxed way of life. A fantastic variety of beautiful and varied scenery, changing with the seasons, is crammed into the Island, which measures only 23 miles by 13 miles. The Island offers formidable hills, towering cliffs, river valleys, marshes, rich farmland, a variety of woodlands, prehistoric burial mounds, ancient churches, attractive villages, and a wealth of inns and pubs. Criss-crossed by over 500 miles of footpaths and bridleways, as well as additional paths across access land, it also boasts nature reserves, forests, and the most spectacular beaches in the south of England. Half the coastline is a Heritage Coast, an award bestowed on only the very best stretches of shoreline in the country, and more than 50% of the Island has been designated as an Area of Outstanding Natural Beauty. Small wonder then, that the Island is one of the best walking venues in England, and no accident that it is home to the UK's biggest walking festival, perfect, as it is, for a day trip walking expedition from the mainland.

GETTING THERE AND GETTING ABOUT

For foot passengers from the mainland, Stagecoach Buses (www.stagecoachbus.com /south), have a 'Triplelink' day ticket option, which includes unlimited travel on their buses, a crossing on the Wightlink Fastcat from **Portsmouth** to **Ryde**, a trip down the half-mile long pier on Island Trains,

Stagecoach Coastliner bus N°700

Wightlink FastCat passenger ferry

and unlimited bus travel on Southern Vectis buses on the Island. This is a terrific deal for a day out from the mainland without the car.

Wightlink (www.wightlink.co.uk) run the Fastcat foot passenger service from **Portsmouth** to **Ryde**, and car ferries from **Portsmouth** to **Fishbourne**, and **Lymington** to **Yarmouth**.

Special deals for a car and passengers are readily available, and a day trip provides for an inexpensive and perfect introduction to the amazing and perhaps under-appreciated, walking possibilities that the Island has to offer.

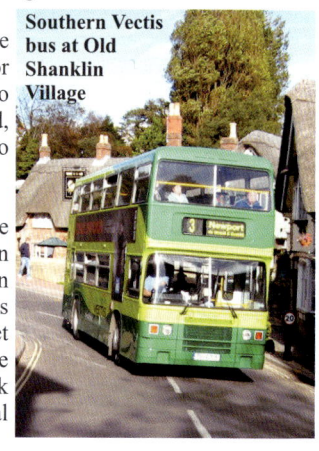

Southern Vectis bus at Old Shanklin Village

For those staying on the Island, and those fortunate enough to live here, Southern Vectis Buses (www.islandbuses.info), run services across the entire Island. All walks are accessible by bus. A 'Freedom 7' ticket at £20 will give unlimited bus travel on the Island for seven days - a real bargain! Park the car and forget it for a week! The best deal of all, a free bus pass, is only available to those fortunate Island residents over 60 - a complimentary ticket to some of the best walking in the UK.

CREATION OF THE ISLAND

All the rocks on the Island are sedimentary in origin, formed in the most recent 1% of the history of the earth, and all being created under water. The oldest rocks, Wealden, appear on the south west coast from **Compton Bay** to **Atherfield**, and at **Sandown**. They were laid down about 110 million years ago, when the area was part of a large river estuary, and often contain the bones of reptiles and dinosaurs. As the land sank and the sea deepened, additional layers of sandstone and clay were formed. These underlay the southern half of the Island until, 100 to 75 million years ago, it was covered by a 500 metre deep sea, and the chalk hills, which now form the backbone of the Island, were created. Microscopic algae were eaten by tiny shrimp-like creatures, whose excrement sank to the sea bed. Hence we have the slightly startling probability that chalk derives from shrimp droppings! We could imagine that the sea was a cloudy white soup. In fact, the chalk formed very slowly - in a human lifetime of, say, 75 years, only one millimetre of ooze would have been formed.

Fossil shells in sea-eroded rocks at Thorness Bay

Around 70 million years ago the sea bed gradually rose to become land, being eroded over time before slipping beneath the sea again under warmer and shallower seas. A younger sediment of softer material was deposited 55 to 35 million years ago as layers of sands and clays which now cover the northern half of the Island and are clearly visible in the cliffs of **Alum Bay** and **Whitecliff Bay**.

As the earth's crust heaved and buckled some 30 million years ago, pressure from the African continent, as it pushed against Europe, folded and lifted the chalk bed. Weathering and rivers cut into the chalk until, in the Ice Age of 2 million to 14,000 years ago, water from thawing snow and ice carved valleys into the frozen chalk, forming many of the dry valleys we see today. Erosion continued, and as the great ice sheets melted, the sea levels rose, eventually inundating what is now the **Solent**, and separating what became the Isle of Wight from the mainland around 8,000 years ago.

Fissures opening up above Compton Bay

As we walk around the coastline it soon becomes apparent that there is an alarming amount of coastal erosion, some caused by wave action, but the majority caused by land slipping into the sea, usually on a bed of blue slipper clay, lubricated by copious amounts of rainfall. Fossil hunters are well-rewarded, while walkers witness the fascinating power of nature at close quarters.

MAN ON THE ISLAND

The Long Stone
(Walks 6 & 9)

Only during warmer phases of the Ice Ages could nomadic hunters roam, and flint implements from Palaeolithic times have been found on the Island. Around 12,000 years ago, as the tundra thawed, the bare landscape very slowly transformed as trees became established. Wild animals moved north, crossing the land bridge, which joined England with that which is now France, and fish became abundant in rivers. The supply of food brought the hunter-gatherers, followed by the first herder farmers of the Neolithic Age (5000 – 1900 BC), with clearance of trees from the thin downland soil being easier than anywhere else. The Neolithic farmers left relatively few marks on the landscape - only three field monuments survive, the most notable being the long barrow known as **The Long Stone** , near **Mottistone**. The other two are a long barrow on **Afton Down**, and a mortuary enclosure on **Tennyson Down**.

Five Barrows (Walks 4 & 5)

Around 240 Bronze Age (1900 – 600 BC) round barrows have been recorded, mostly on the high Downs. Nearly all show signs of looting, either after Henry III's Charter of 1237, which required all barrows to be dug for treasure for the Royal coffers, or by Victorian plunderers. The Iron Age settlements (from about 550 BC) are demonstrated by the occasional field systems, the only major site being **Chillerton Down** hill fort, also occupied by subsequent Roman settlement.

The Romans occupied the Island from 50 – 450 AD, a time of agricultural growth, as the Roman Empire required large amounts of food and fodder. On the back of this, at least seven Roman villas were built, probably by wealthy Romanized British farmers. When the Roman era ended, the Island was dominated by the Jutes, until the West Saxons took over, and Christianity arrived, though pagan beliefs had survived longer here than in any other part of Britain. A period of unrest between the Anglo-Saxons and Viking marauders ensued, with Alfred the Great's forces the victors in a sea battle at Brading. After the Norman conquest of 1066, **Carisbrooke Castle** was built, together with a number

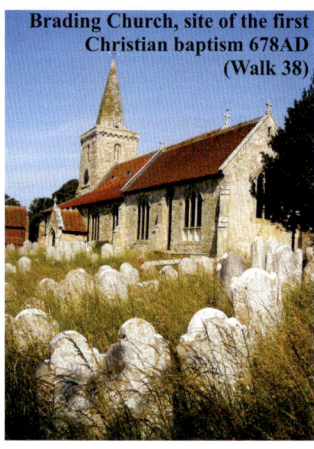
Brading Church, site of the first Christian baptism 678AD
(Walk 38)

of churches. In the fourteenth to the sixteenth centuries, the Island was frequently under attack from French raiding parties, and a number of towns were totally destroyed. In the English Civil War (1642-8), the Island was put on the map when Charles 1st was imprisoned in **Carisbrooke Castle**. The British Navy began to exert heavy influence on the Island. In 1782 the Royal George was wrecked, with great loss of life. Should you go rowing on **Ryde** boating lake, you will be floating over the remains of 800 dead from the wreck! Around 1860 a massive program of fortifications was carried out, with four sea forts on the **Solent** built as defence for **Portsmouth**, and land forts built around the Island at **Forts Victoria**, **Albert**, **Golden Hill**, **Bembridge**, **Sandown**, and **The Needles**, as well as a number of other gun batteries. It was at this time that the west of the Island became more accessible, with the construction of the **Military Road**. With the coming of the railways, and Queen Victoria spending a great deal of her year here, the Island became a tourist destination, as it has remained to this day.

FLORA & FAUNA

Separation from the mainland has given the Island a slightly different range of flora and fauna. Some species are absent, such as grey squirrel, deer (extinct on the Island 200 years ago), sand lizard, nuthatch and tawny owl. It also boasts a few species unique to the UK- wall lizards, the Glanville fritillary butterfly, and two plants, wood calamint and wild columbine.

Pyramid Orchid, Shide Quarry (Walk 26)

There is a wealth of wild flowers: primrose, celandine, wood anemone, bluebell, and the distinctive garlic aroma of the ramson - all common in spring woodland. The arrival of summer is heralded by the red campion, which adorns woodland edges, and the majestic foxglove in woodland clearings. The open downland displays cowslips, pyramid orchids, bird's-foot trefoil. In fact, up to 40 different plants can be found in a square yard of chalk downland turf.

Clouded Yellow butterfly (Walk 29)

Twenty-seven species of orchid have been recorded, the pyramidal orchid being the Island's flower. Along the south west coast and **The Needles**, there is a stunning display of thrift in spring, and the heathland glows purple with heather in August.

This range of plants and habitats attracts a wide variety of butterflies, from the first flights of brimstones and orange tips, the early summer marbled white and the beautiful blues, to the occasional

Chalkhill Blue on Tennyson Down (Walk 1)

continental invasion of the clouded yellow in late summer. A good butterfly identification book is a 'must', to appreciate the number of species, ever changing as spring progresses to autumn.

Walkers will often hear the laughing cackle of the green woodpecker, the clattering wings of the wood pigeon, the unexpected raucous croak of the pheasant – enough to startle even the most intrepid explorer, and occasionally the whirring wings of the partridge. Not so long ago, to see or hear a buzzard was a rare occurrence. Now, they are common, with their distinctive mewing call.

Thrift on the south-west coast (Walk 6)

A variety of ducks, geese and waders can be seen around the coasts, as well as migrating ospreys around the **Newtown Nature Reserve**. One of the most impressive birds is the raven, unusual in the south of England, but relatively common here, with its unmistakable deep guttural call, mainly found along the south and west coasts. The best spots for migratory birds are **St. Catherine's Lighthouse** in the spring, and **Fort Victoria** in the late summer and autumn. In November I had the surreal experience of watching a snow bunting on **Luccombe Down**, as a red admiral butterfly fluttered by! When crossing on the ferry, it is not unusual to see the occasional gannet and other migrating sea birds.

If you are lucky, you may see an adder basking in the sun, and there is a fair chance of sighting a fox running across a field. They were introduced in the 18th century for the foxhunting fraternity. Voles and shrews are common, with their high-pitched squeaks - unlike children, heard and not seen! Weasels and stoats may be seen, and rabbits are common (introduced by the Normans, **Thorley** was a huge rabbit warren). Badgers are plentiful, although you will probably have to become nocturnal to spot one. The Isle of Wight is very proud to have a large population of red squirrels inhabiting the woodlands and forests, a shy creature, and much harder to spot than the mainland grey variety. Perhaps the biggest delight of all remains the sighting of a hare at close quarters - a truly beautiful mammal.

THE WALKS

The walks in this book are the best the Island can offer. Every one has something special - all have an element of wow-factor, and all have a pub on the route! Each walk has been thoroughly researched, to ensure accurate and, dare I say it, foolproof directions. The walks are suited to both car owners, and bus users (all the walks were researched using Southern Vectis buses). For GPS converts, precise, easily downloadable, routes from the Discovery

Walking Guides PNF CD can be used in association with this book.

Fingerpost showing path V28 (Walk 33)

I've avoided walks through built up areas and in the north east of the Island, where no network of suitable footpaths exists, and I have tried to avoid road walking as much as possible. All the routes have been carefully chosen to use the very best paths of the various Island Trails, and to avoid the not so good ones. Where a path number appears in the text (i.e BS26), it is always taken from an actual fingerpost on the route. GPS signals are good on all routes, although there will be the occasional wooded area where a dense leaf canopy shields signals in summer. The timings between waypoints serve as a guide only.

We all walk at varying speeds, and I do not include stops to admire views etc.

I have deliberately avoided the use of the term ´way post´ or 'way marker', to avoid confusion with waypoints, using marker post instead. Be aware that not all junctions of bridleways and footpaths have finger or marker posts, many are completely unmarked.

Finally, before you venture forth into this amazing landscape, a word on access land. We all welcome the opportunity to walk on new land, but it is worth noting that landowners may restrict access rights for 28 days a year for any reason (see www.countrysideaccess.gov.uk). Finally, Southern Vectis bus numbers were correct at time of going to press, but are liable to change from time to time.

ORDNANCE SURVEY MAPPING

All the map sections which accompany the detailed walk descriptions in Walk! the Isle of Wight are reproduced under Ordnance Survey licence from the digital versions of the latest Explorer 1:25,000 scale maps. Each map section is then re-scaled to 30,000 scale to fit our book design layout. Discovery Walking Guide's Walking Routes and GPS Waypoints are then drawn onto the map section to produce the map illustrating each detailed walk description.

The map sections in Walk! The Isle of Wight map are sufficient for following the detailed walk descriptions, but for planning your adventures in this region we strongly recommend that you purchase the latest OS Explorer maps.

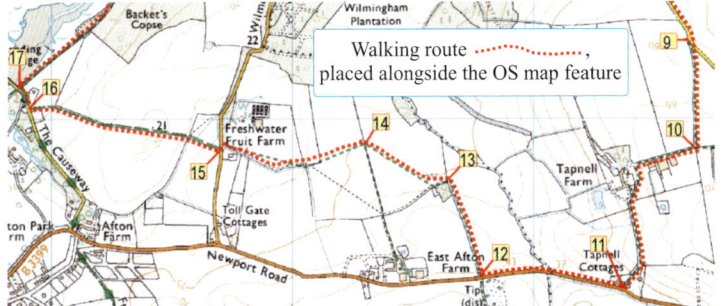

Walking route ·············, placed alongside the OS map feature

Isle of Wight

Cow

Yarmouth

Totland

Cowes

East Cowes

Ryde

34

25

31

39

Newport

Bembridge

26

37

29

38

21

35

40

24

Sandown

30

33

Shanklin

28

36

32

22

27

23

Ventnor

The **GPS Waypoint Lists** provided in **Walk! The Isle Of Wight** are as recorded by Martin Simons while researching the detailed walk descriptions for this book. On the map section(s) for each walking route the **Waypoint Symbols** are numbered so that they can be directly identified with the walk description and **Waypoint List** for that walking route. All GPS Waypoints are subject to the accuracy of GPS units in the particular location of each waypoint. Where there is good GPS satellite reception, which is most of the time, then an accuracy of 5 metres can be expected.

Across the beautiful landscapes of the Isle of Wight GPS reception is generally excellent for the majority of Martin's walking routes. Occasional exceptions to 'excellent reception' may occur in woodland, due to signals being blocked by the trunks of trees and dense leaf canopy in summer, and in urban areas where buildings may be blocking the satellite reception.

Satellite Reception
Accurate location fixes for your GPS unit depend upon you receiving signals from four or more satellites. Providing you have good batteries, and that you wait until your gps has full 'satellite acquisition' before starting out, your gps unit will perform well across the Isle of Wight. GPS satellites are not in geo-stationary orbits, as some people believe, meaning that satellite reception at any given point will vary during the day depending upon the satellite configuration at the time.

Manually Inputting Waypoints
GPS Waypoints are quoted for the **OSGB** (Ordnance Survey Great Britain) datum and **BNG** (British National Grid) coordinates, making them identical with the OS grid coordinates of the position they refer to.

To manually input the Waypoints into your GPS unit we suggest that you:

- Switch on your GPS and select 'simulator/standby' mode

- Check that your GPS is set to the OSGB datum and BNG 'location/position format'.

- Input the GPS Waypoints into a 'route' with the same number as the walking route; then when you call up the 'route' on the Isle of Wight there will be no confusion as to which walking route it refers to.

- Repeat the inputting of waypoints into 'routes' until you have covered all the routes you plan to walk, or until you have used up the memory capacity of your GPS.

- Turn off your GPS. When you switch your GPS back on it should return to its normal navigation mode.

Note that the **GPS Waypoints** complement the routes in **Walk! The Isle of Wight** and are not intended as an alternative to the detailed walk descriptions.

Personal Navigator Files (PNFs) CD version 4.01 onwards

Edited versions of Martin Simons' original GPS research tracks and waypoints are available as downloadable files on our PNFs CD from version 4.01 onwards. Our PNFs CD includes all the edited GPS Tracks and Waypoints for all the Walk! Guide books published by DWG along with Google Earth files of our walking routes and GPS Utility Special Edition software. See DWG websites for more information.

www.walking.demon.co.uk & www.dwgwalking.co.uk

GPS The Easy Way (updated 2nd edition)

If you are confused by talk of GPS, but are interested in how this modern navigational aid could enhance your walking enjoyment, then simply seek out a copy of GPS The Easy Way. At £4.99 its a 'pocket money' investment for everyone thinking about buying a GPS unit. Written in easy to understand, jargon-free, terms this little book has helped thousands of walkers to understand GPS units and their use for walking navigation.

Discovery Walking Guides Ltd.
10 Tennyson Close
Northampton NN5 7HJ
www.walking.demon.co.uk www.dwgwalking.co.uk

SYMBOLS RATING GUIDE

 our rating for effort/exertion:-
1 very easy **2** easy **3** average
4 energetic **5** strenuous

 approximate **time** to complete a walk (compare your times against ours early in a walk) - does not include stopping time

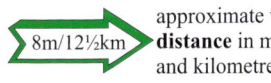 approximate walking **distance** in miles and kilometres

 approximate **ascents/descents** in metres (N=negligible)

 **circular** route

 **linear** route

 **figure of eight** route

 risk of **vertigo**

 refreshments (may be at start or end of a route only)

Walk descriptions include:

- timing in minutes, shown as (40M)
- compass directions, shown as (NW)
- heights in metres, shown as (1355m)
- GPS waypoints, shown as (Wp.3)

Notes on the text

Place names are shown in **bold text**, except where we refer to a written sign, when they are enclosed in single quotation marks.

WALKING EQUIPMENT

A good pair of boots is the best investment you can make. My Brasher Hillmasters are still going strong after 10 years, teamed with a pair of quality walking socks. A 'grippy' sole is essential to cope with slippery slopes (wet chalk can be like walking on ice), and dry, crumbly slopes are equally hazardous. Gaiters may be a useful addition, particularly in winter, or after heavy dew.

Being of a frugal disposition, I wear what I find comfortable and affordable. My apparel is based on thin layers under a zip-up fleece jacket, multi-pocketed trousers, and a seasonal hat (essential for the follicly challenged like me). Even when the ground is frozen, once walking and climbing, I find I am self-heating. The only coat I wear is a pouch-sized breathable waterproof, donned if necessary, to keep out wind and rain. Extreme weather is unusual on the Island, unless you are a glutton for punishment and go looking for it, and I like to walk with minimum clutter. A small rucksack with water, waterproofs, chocolate and a banana, sunscreen, lip salve, elastoplast, small binoculars, spare GPS batteries, a whistle if on my own, a compass that I have never yet had occasion to use, and a mobile phone with a fully charged battery (note that mobile phones do not work in some areas). A yellow high visibility waistcoat is strongly advised where walking on any busy or fast road.

Warm summer days encourage the wearing of shorts, though nettles can be a problem. The answer is to carry a small pair of secateurs to cut and trim a suitable beating stick, with which to thrash them into submission!

One final tip: picture the scene as you arrive at a pub with wet and muddy boots. You soil your hands taking them off to leave outside, then worry that someone is going to steal them leaving you stranded in your socks! A pair of Tesco carrier bags is the perfect remedy. Put your foot in, tie the handles together and away you go. Perhaps not for the fashion icons among you, but it certainly works!

1. Tennyson Down and The Needles

A climb up beautiful **Tennyson Down** rewards with stunning views before a fine cliff top path takes us to a Cold War rocket engine testing site. Passing fortifications from Victoria to WWII, on a panoramic path with views across **Alum Bay** and beyond, we return to downland slopes, and then visit a rare long barrow on the heathland of **Headon Hill**. The **Highdown Inn** offers refreshment before we return through woodland to **Freshwater Bay**.

4 | 3H | 8 miles/12.9km | 350m / 350m | ⚠ | ↻ | 3 🍴

Short Walk

From **Tennyson's Monument** Wp.3, turn away from the sea on a descending footpath through the trees which drops down around the right side of a disued pit by a car park, turn right to join the homeward leg at Wp.17. (1 hour 15mins, 3 miles/4.8km)

Access by bus: No.7 to **Freshwater Bay**
Access by car: Freshwater Bay car park behind the seafront.

From the bus stops (Wp.1 0M), west of the seafront, we turn up a private road signed 'Fort Redoubt'(if the path ahead is closed for repairs follow the diversion route on the right which rejoins the walk at Wp.2). As the road turns left, we keep ahead on the **Coastal Path** through a gate, passing above **Watcombe Bay** and climbing to pass through a kissing gate (Wp.2 13M). With a choice of paths up **Tennyson Down**, we favour the cliff top route for superior walking pleasure, joined by fulmars and gulls effortlessly gliding on the thermal updrafts with towering Channel views.

the 'Adventurous' cliff-top pat

The **Tennyson Monument**, an Iona cross made of Cornish granite, is inscribed 'In memory of Alfred Lord

Tennyson Monument

Tennyson this cross is raised. A beacon to sailors by the people of Freshwater and other friends in England and America'. The view from the Monument is superb across the **Solent**, **West Wight**, **Hurst Castle** and the distant Dorset coast.

Needles viewpoint

From the **Monument** (Wp.3 31M), we head west (turn inland for the short walk), winding down to cross the left stile (Wp.4 40M) to walk on the sea side of a fence along the unprotected and more adventurous cliff top path. At the fence end, near a transmitter aerial, we keep on the cliff top path with **The Needles** coming into view. Dropping sharply down to a concrete road (Wp.5 69M), we turn right, passing through the Black Knight and Black Arrow rocket engine testing site of the 1956-1971 Cold War era. Keeping right up a fork (left to visit a Needles viewpoint), we climb up passing a Coastguard lookout. We turn left before a World War 2 gun battery (Wp.6 72M), up, then down steps on a path signed 'Needles Old Battery 1862' to a road (Wp.7 77M).

view to Alum Bay

To visit the Battery, the highlight of which is the narrowest of spiral staircases to a tunnel leading to a searchlight position overlooking **The Needles**, turn left at the road.

We turn right, on a rising road, soon walking on the raised left verge, with spectacular views of the coloured sandstone cliffs of **Alum Bay**. Our path leaves the road, veering left down a fine chalky path across the open cliff tops, eventually rejoining the road and bearing left. As the road swings left down to the raucous clamour of **Alum Bay**, we continue ahead up concrete steps (Wp.8 94M) and over a stile, maintaining direction along the lower slopes of the Downs. **Headon Hill**, with its long barrow clearly silhouetted is on the skyline to the left, as we loosely follow the left hedge line, tempted by the entrance gate to **Warren Farm** Cream Teas.

Opposite a disused chalk pit, we turn left (Wp.9 104M), crossing a stile onto a hedge enclosed path, before descending an access track, turning left along the

verge of the main road (Wp.10 108M). Crossing the road, we turn right over a stile by a fingerpost onto T16 (Wp.11 110M), climbing a grassy track and passing a round barrow on the right. Over a stile, we climb to pass a fingerpost (fingerless at the time of writing) (Wp.12 116M), turning left on a wide, rabbit cropped, grass path, overlooking **Hurst Castle** across the **Solent**. We follow

Highdown Inn

the path up to the west side of the Bronze Age long barrow (1500BC), on top of the hill. Circling round the fence and turning half right (Wp.13 121M) to drop down the heather clad slopes onto a path leading us back along the hillside, completing the loop as we return to pass the fingerpost (Wp.12 126M). Maintaining direction, on a wide descending path through gorse, then down a shady tree tunnel, we cross two stiles, emerging at a road (Wp.14 134M). Turning right, we cross to go over a fingerpost stile on T28, crossing a field to go over another stile and turning left along a narrow road (Wp.15 137M). By a double bend, we turn right, up **Highdown Lane** (Wp.16 141M), or visit the **Highdown Inn** (Highdown was the original name for **Tennyson Down**).

At the top of the lane, we turn left just before a car park (Wp.17 145M), soon on a wide grass path by an attractive pit, which funnels into an underdown woodland. Going through a kissing gate, the delightful edge of woodland path, with pleasing glimpses across the **Solent**, takes us past a marker post and then another large chalk pit. By the next marker post (Wp.18 156M), we fork right, taking the upper path, gradually climbing up through the trees to emerge on the north side of **Tennyson Down** (Wp.19 160M). Keeping left, we follow the grass path along the top edge of the woodland, until our path bears left, away from the sea. Descending twixt tree and hedge to a fingerpost T-junction (Wp.20 169M), we turn right, emerging through a field gate and following the left fence down a meadow. Before a footpath gate (Wp.21 171M), we turn right, still following the left fence line, then keeping ahead to pass to the right of a fir tree. Following the left fence line, passing through a gate, we turn right by **Dimbola Lodge** (Wp.22 174M), to return down the footway to the bus stops (Wp.1 177M), or continue down to **Freshwater Bay** for refreshments.

Once the Isle of Freshwater, cut off from the rest of the Island by tidal marshes, before the causeway was built from **Yarmouth**. The Victorian fortifications of the Palmerston era are particularly evident in the Western tip of the Island. Our walk takes us past two of the Forts, with a third, **Fort Albert**, hidden by trees.

This varied walk takes us along the Solent shoreline, through **Fort Victoria** and **Golden Hill Country Parks** before winding through **Afton Marsh** to the attractive **Freshwater Bay**. We return over the foothills of **Afton Down**, passing the impressive **Old Freshwater Church** and the **Red Lion Inn**, to cross a tree and farm landscape back to the charming town of **Yarmouth**.

Short Walks:
(a) From **Yarmouth** follow the route to Wp.9, turning left behind the school. Keep ahead on the path, emerging to join a road by a Post Office and maintaining direction across a junction to the **Red Lion Inn** Wp.25. (2 hours 10mins, 5.7 miles/9.2km).
(b) From **Freshwater Bay** Wp.16, follow the route past the **Red Lion** Wp.25. Maintain direction across a road junction, turning right onto footpath F66, soon after the Post Office. Re-join the route by turning left at Wp.9 behind the school. (1 hour 10mins, 3.1 miles/5km)

Access by bus: No.7 to **Yarmouth**, or **Freshwater Bay** for short walk (b).
Access by car: Car park opposite the harbour at **Yarmouth**, or behind **Freshwater Bay** for short walk (b).

From the bus station (Wp.1 0M), we head west, away from the town, crossing the road bridge over the **Western Yar**, and passing the quaintly named **Gasworks Lane**. At a sharp bend we turn right on the **Coastal Path** (Wp.2 9M), soon turning left along the fine sea wall, with lovely views over the Solent. As the wall ends we continue along the foreshore, passing around the outside of **Fort Victoria**.

Soon after rounding the point, passing a carved dolphin (Wp.3 22M), we veer away from the sea to join a path at the edge of the woods by a green and white Nature Trail sign. Climbing into the woodland, and ignoring all crossing paths, we turn right at a T-junction on the **Coastal Path** (Wp.4 25M), along the wide, beautifully surfaced woodland track, with tantalizing glimpses of the sea. Bearing left up a flight of steps, we take the main path, leaving **Fort Victoria Country Park** on a tarmac footpath, which turns left between fences to pass a holiday park with views across **Colwell Bay**. At an

Comma Butterfly

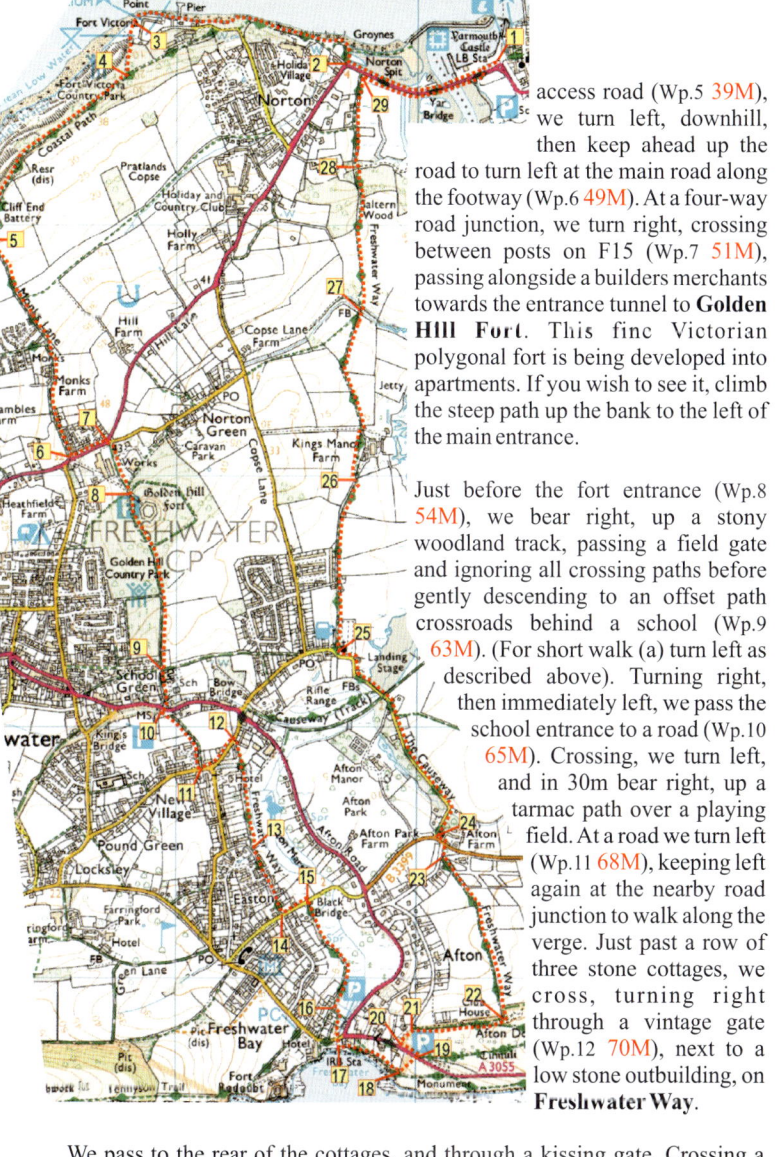

access road (Wp.5 39M), we turn left, downhill, then keep ahead up the road to turn left at the main road along the footway (Wp.6 49M). At a four-way road junction, we turn right, crossing between posts on F15 (Wp.7 51M), passing alongside a builders merchants towards the entrance tunnel to **Golden Hill Fort**. This fine Victorian polygonal fort is being developed into apartments. If you wish to see it, climb the steep path up the bank to the left of the main entrance.

Just before the fort entrance (Wp.8 54M), we bear right, up a stony woodland track, passing a field gate and ignoring all crossing paths before gently descending to an offset path crossroads behind a school (Wp.9 63M). (For short walk (a) turn left as described above). Turning right, then immediately left, we pass the school entrance to a road (Wp.10 65M). Crossing, we turn left, and in 30m bear right, up a tarmac path over a playing field. At a road we turn left (Wp.11 68M), keeping left again at the nearby road junction to walk along the verge. Just past a row of three stone cottages, we cross, turning right through a vintage gate (Wp.12 70M), next to a low stone outbuilding, on **Freshwater Way**.

We pass to the rear of the cottages, and through a kissing gate. Crossing a small meadow, we go over a plank bridge and stile, and through a well-tended garden, which we leave over another stile, along an enclosed path, with **Afton Marsh** on our left. Crossing two more stiles, we turn left along a road (Wp.13 76M) and then left again at a road junction (Wp.14 78M). In 110m we turn right by a fingerpost on F36 (Wp.15 80M), up a track, then a path, through the Marsh - a lovely path, which includes a board walk. After two kissing gates, we emerge on an access road by the **Sandpipers Hotel**, with a refreshment opportunity at the **Fat Cat Bar**.

We turn left immediately before the Bar by a

Freshwater Bay

fingerpost on F52 (Wp.16 87M), soon turning right through a kissing gate to pass through two car parks, before carefully crossing the road onto **Freshwater Bay** promenade (Wp.17 90M). Turning left along the attractive seafront, we climb a flight of wooden steps to join the **Coastal Path**, passing along the cliff top with charming backward views across the Bay. As we pass the last bungalow (Wp.18 97M), we turn left on a weaving grass path, to cross the **Military Road**, turning left down the verge (Wp.19 98M). Bearing right before the bus stop (Wp.20 99M), up an access road, we bear right by a fingerpost up F32 (Wp.21 100M), passing a golf clubhouse. By another fingerpost (Wp.22 106M), we bear left down F32, keeping left again down to a fingerpost onto F31. We pass between fields as we leave the lower slopes of **Afton Down**.

The Causeway

Through a gate (Wp.23 113M), we turn right

Red Lion & Old Freshwater Church

along an access road, crossing the nearby main road, and turning left, then right down The Causeway (Wp.24 115M). This unimpressive road eventually redeems itself, as we cross a fine stone causeway and bridge across the upper reaches of the **River Yar**, with **Old Freshwater Church** on the hill ahead. Continuing up the road we reach the church, an atmospheric building, with beautiful, massive, nave columns. Conveniently next to the church is the **Red Lion Inn**, dating back to the 11th century, with flagstone floor, perhaps one of the Island's best pubs - fine food and a log fire in winter. (For short walk (b) continue along the road as above).

We take the path twixt pub and church (Wp.25 131M), F1, crossing two stiles and maintaining direction along a tarmac access road, with the **Western Yar** nestling below on our right. Just before **Kings Manor Farm**, by a fingerpost, we cross a double stile bridge (Wp.26 139M), turning right, over a field, to go over another stile. An enclosed woodland path emerges through a kissing gate and we bear left up a wide undulating farm track. Dropping down to a wooded dip, we turn half right, leaving the track to cross a stile and bridge by a fingerpost (Wp.27 147M). Over another stile, we emerge to pass up the left edge of a field to cross a stile onto a path between fields. At the top of a rise, with a final look back to the distant Downs, we cross a stile and plunge down a woodland path. At a post and rail fence by a fingerpost (Wp.28 156M), we turn left on a substantial access road, **Gasworks Lane**, taking us back to the main road (Wp.29 160M) where we turn right to return to sample the delights of **Yarmouth** (Wp.1 165M).

3. The Western Yar & Yarmouth

I confess I had doubts over this walk at the planning stage, but in practice it turned out an extremely enjoyable route, on very quiet, and in some cases 'invisible' paths. Starting through old **Yarmouth** and along the sea wall, we head inland on the old railway line and through the lovely **Mill Copse**. Looping round through an undulating agricultural landscape to the **River Yar**, we return along the railway line to the salt marsh and harbour.

Yarmouth is over 1000 years old, the closest town to the mainland, and best described as an 'old fashioned' port, with a unique atmosphere.

3 | 3H | 7.8 miles/12.6km | 135m / 135m | 3

Short Walk: Very short walk through Yarmouth, along the sea wall, through Rofford Marsh, turning right at Wp.6 to to return through the harbour. (45 mins, 1.9 miles/3.1km)

Access by bus: No.7 to **Yarmouth** bus station.
Access by car: Car park opposite the harbour.

From **Yarmouth** bus station (Wp.1 0M), we pass the bus shelter and information office, crossing the ferry access road to go along a no entry one-way street, and past the **Wheatsheaf Inn** towards the church. At a T-junction we bear left (Wp.2 2M), then right into the narrow High Street. Maintaining direction across two junctions, we turn left at **Yarmouth Common** (Wp.3 6M) to walk along the top of the sea wall alongside the **Solent**. Ignoring the **Coastal Path** fingerpost, we keep to the sea wall, turning right 10 metres after the end of a fence and up a flight of steps (Wp.4 12M).

Yarmouth Mill from railway track

White Admiral seen on railway track

Crossing the busy main road, we go down **Thorley Road**, turning right soon after the entrance to **Rofford House** onto the old railway line by a hard to spot fingerpost (Wp.5 15M). The track takes us across **Rofford Marsh** and through the old **Yarmouth** railway station, with wildlife rich ponds to our left. At a 4-way fingerpost (Wp.6 31M), we bear left on Y1 through a kissing gate to pass through the lovely Nature Reserve of 400 year old **Mill Copse**. Keeping ahead on the main path, we emerge through a kissing gate, turning right to follow the left fence line with fine views across to the Downs. This delightful lightly wooded path emerges, climbing between fences, along a low ridge to a road (Wp.7 49M). Crossing, still on Y1, we go cross-country before turning right along a very quiet road (Wp.8 59M).

There is a proposal for six 100m tall wind turbines here, which has aroused huge local opposition, but would be an awe inspiring sight should it come to fruition.

Soon after cresting the slope, with the Downs ahead, we turn right, crossing a stile by a fingerpost (Wp.9 68M), onto Y9, an invisible path, taking the indicated direction to cross a stile to the left of the farm buildings (Wp.10 76M). Turning right, we pass through **Tapnell Farm**, bearing left along a concrete access and down to a road where we turn right (Wp.11 83M). At a fingerpost (Wp.12 88M), we turn right on F27, crossing a stile onto another invisible path, making for an isolated copse on the left edge of a large meadow. At the far end of the copse, we turn left over a stile (Wp.13 92M), passing through newly planted trees and over a stile in the fence ahead.

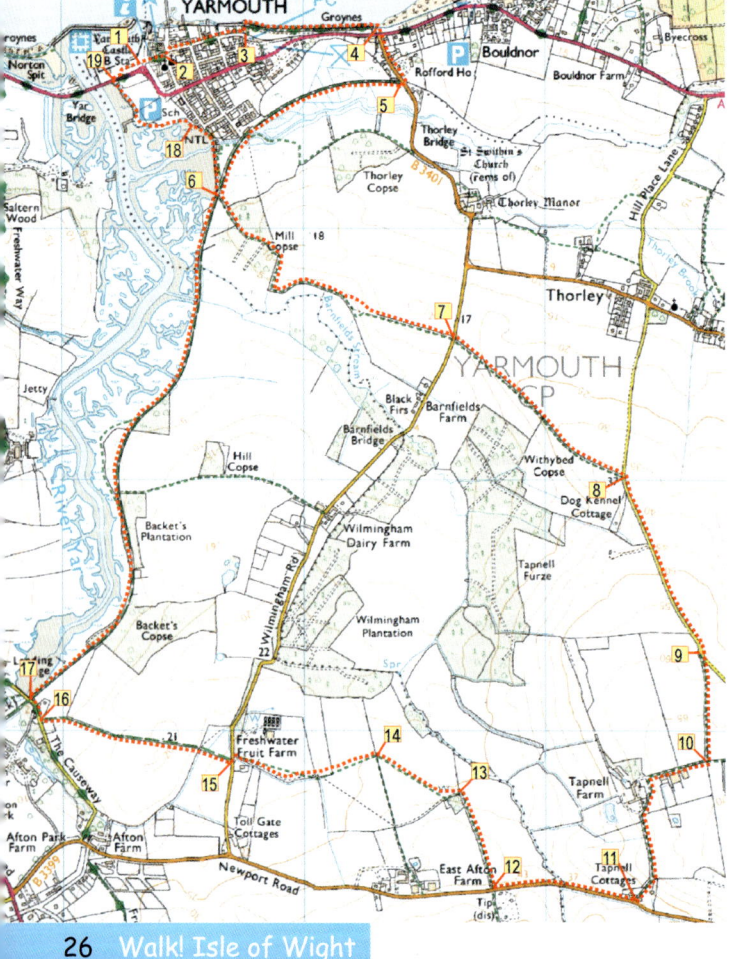

Looking across the Salt Marsh to Yarmouth

Maintaining direction, we make for another stile, isolated in the middle of the next field (Wp.14 102M), turning half left towards another stile near the left end of a hedge-line. Crossing, we pass through the top of a meadow, to go through a gap in a row of fir trees, keeping ahead to follow another line of fir trees on our left. The path becomes apparent as we go through a wood, emerging onto a narrow access road, where we turn left, soon crossing a road to a fingerpost onto F25 (Wp.15 111M). Passing over a low hill, with **Old Freshwater Church** appearing ahead, we turn right at a road (Wp.16 120M) toward the Causeway. (For a refreshment break at the **Red Lion Inn**, cross the bridge and go up the hill to the pub by the church).

We turn right before the picturesque bridge, on F61 (Wp.17 121M), along the old railway track. Our path takes in a wildlife paradise, passing along the banks of the river before becoming tree enclosed, with intermittent views across the salt marsh, before opening out as we approach **Yarmouth**.

Yarmouth Mill from the harbour

We return to the 4-way fingerpost, turning left through the nearby footpath gate, and passing **Yarmouth Tide Mill** (c1793). Keeping left (Wp.18 162M), along the attractive waterside path all the way around the harbour edge to the road bridge (Wp.19 169M), we turn right to return to the bus station (Wp.1 171M), or a choice of **Yarmouth** pubs and tea-rooms for refreshments.

4. Compton Down and Five Barrows

A lovely West Wight walk from the charming **Freshwater Bay** along the high Downs to the unforgettable **Five Barrows** on **Brook Down**. Descending to the coast, we return along the stunning, sometimes scary, cliff top path. Wonderful views all the way!

Short Walk: For **Freshwater Bay**, **Afton Down** and the scary cliffs, turn right at Wp.4 descending to the **Military Road** and turn right along the cliff top Coastal Path to return. (1 hour. 2.5 miles / 4km)

Access by bus: No 7 to **Freshwater Bay**.
Access by car: Car park opposite the seafront at **Freshwater Bay**.

Freshwater Esplanade

From the bus stop we make our way to the seafront (Wp.1 0M), by the **Albion Hotel**, turning left along the esplanade and climbing a flight of wooden steps. We follow the cliff top path until, after passing the last bungalow (Wp.2 7M), we turn left on a grass path winding to the **Military Road**. We cross to a fingerpost (Wp.3 8M), turning right up F33, the **Tennyson Trail**. The track steadily climbs **Afton Down** to a junction of tracks (Wp.4 18M) (bear right, downhill for short walk), where we keep climbing ahead across **Compton Down**, with fine views to the **Solent** and the south west coast. Crossing a stile (Wp.5 41M), we leave the golf course, continuing along the gorse clad downland tops. As we approach the unmistakable **Five Barrows** (Wp.6 60M), atop **Brook Down**, we branch left to visit this mystical

Compton Down looking East

Five Barrows looking West

collection of barrows, with amazing panoramic views. In fact there are eight Bronze Age barrows, six bowl, a bell on the west side, and a disc on the east side. Dropping down, initially heading towards distant **Brook** church, we join the main track, turning left and then bearing right (Wp.7 63M), descending round the top of an attractive disused chalk pit. Following a track across the pit floor, we merge with a substantial track (Wp.8 66M), which joins from our left. Keeping left by a blue sign 'BS89', we descend the track through scrub, curving to the left and passing through a field gate. Before a fingerpost by a field gate (Wp.9 71M), we turn left, immediately keeping right up onto a raised grass path, above a track which curves away left. This superb, slightly sunken, path descends between sparse trees towards **Dunsbury Farm**, where, after passing through two field gates, we turn right on a tarmac road (Wp.10 76M). This leads us past farm buildings on BS86, before becoming a sandy track. At a dip, immediately before a small wood, **Grange Withy Bed**, we turn left (Wp.11 85M), down a grassy farm track to a farmhouse. Turning right at a T-junction (Wp.12 92M), and crossing a cattle grid, we continue to the **Military Road** (Wp.13 95M), turning left along the verge. We turn right into **Hanover Point** car park (Wp.14 96M), passing down the right side before turning right along the cliff top **Coastal Path** (Wp.15 97M). This fascinating path, with wonderful views to the chalk cliffs of **Freshwater Bay** and astonishing areas of slumped coast, takes us west, with the occasional alarming fissure appearing by the path. Crossing a stile by a

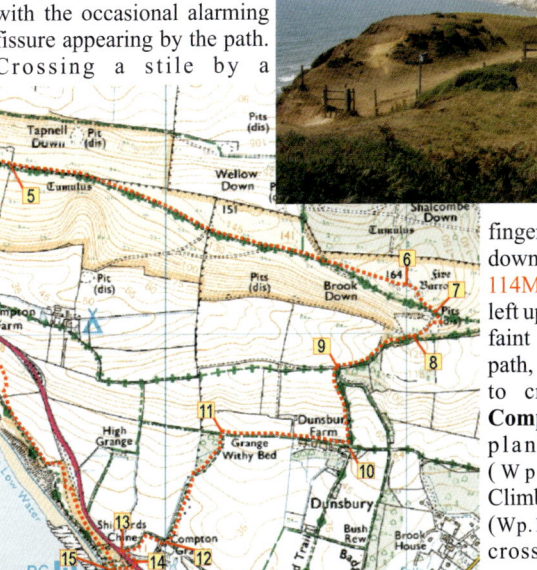
Dropping down to the track

fingerpost, we drop down to a track (Wp.16 114M), soon keeping left up a bank, to join a faint grass cliff top path, then descending to cross the small **Compton Chine** on a plank footbridge (Wp.17 119M). Climbing to a stile (Wp.18 124M), we cross, turning left

Looking East from the high cliff-top path

alongside the road before bearing left to regain the cliff top path (Wp.19 127M). This path must be the scariest on the Island 260 feet high, in close proximity to the edge and with worryingly large cracks! For those of a nervous disposition, there is a safer parallel-path just inland. We eventually drop to rejoin our outward route, descending the wooden steps to return to the esplanade (Wp.1 151M), for refreshments at the kiosk, **Albion Hotel**, tearoom, or quirky **Fat Cat Bar**, at the rear of the car parks.

5. Hulverstone to Ningwood

The first three miles of this walk are a delight, and the rest isn't bad either! Starting from the **Sun Inn**, we climb up through attractive woodland to a top quality path through heather and gorse overlooking the south coastline. Turning west, a terraced path yields wonderful views toward **Tennyson Down**, before we descend past three round barrows for a strenuous climb to the summit of the fantastic **Five Barrows**. Heading inland we descend the slopes of **Wellow Down**, passing through an arable landscape, **Rossiters Vineyard**, attractive woodland, and across **Ningwood 'Lake'**, to finish at the very fine **Horse and Groom** pub.

3   2¼ H   6.7 miles/10.8km   260m / 300m   4

Access by bus: Bus No 7 to the **Sun Inn**, **Hulverstone** (near **Brighstone**), returning on Bus No 7 from the **Horse and Groom**, **Ningwood** (near **Shalfleet**).
Access by car: Roadside parking at the **Sun Inn**, **Hulverstone**, buses back.

From the **Sun Inn** (Wp.1 0M), we cross the road to go up a shady footpath, passing through a gate and over a stile into a meadow. Keeping ahead, up the meadow edge, we cross another stile, maintaining direction up a lovely rising grass path to cross a stile into woodland. A fabulous path winds up through beech trees on a carpet of autumn leaves to a T-junction (Wp.2 11M), where we turn right. Following

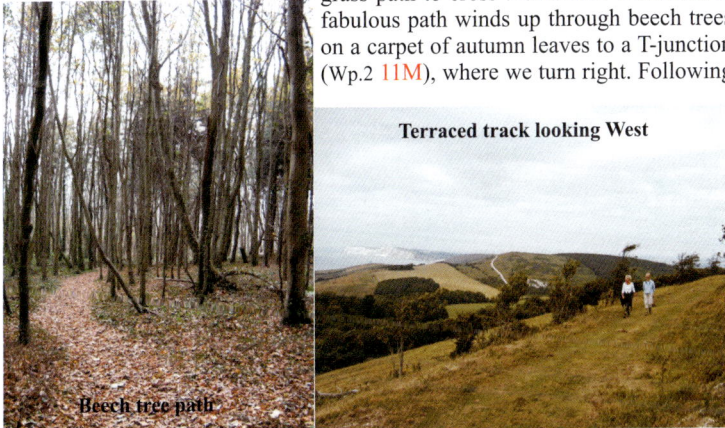

Terraced track looking West

Beech tree path

the main stony track, we weave through bracken, gorse and heather, with wonderful coastal views. Soon after the path starts to descend and curve right, at a grassy clearing, we turn left to go through a kissing gate next to a field gate (Wp.3 16M), rising through light woodland. Emerging through a bridleway gate by a fingerpost (Wp.4 19M), we bear half left up a beautiful, grassy, terraced path, which soon yields superb views west across **Freshwater Bay**. We follow the main path through bushes to two fingerposts, bearing left to join the **Tennyson Trail** (Wp.5 26M) on a downhill track and going through a bridleway gate. Descending to the right of the main track, we pass three round barrows on the slopes of **Pay Down**, with our next destination, **Five Barrows**, silhouetted across the valley ahead. Passing through a field gate, we

Rossiters Vineyard

Agricultural landscape to the Solent

diagonally cross a road (Wp.6 33M), to go up a flinty track by a fingerpost and through a bridleway gate. As the, now chalky, track curves right, we veer right (Wp.7 35M), making our own way through the gorse, as we climb to the summit of **Five Barrows**, one of the Island's special places (see walk 4), with commanding views and a sense of mystery past. Continuing west, we pass the last barrow, gently descending to rejoin the main track. When level with the corner of a wood away to our right, we bear right, away from the sea, on a wide grass path (Wp.8 48M), very loosely following the right fence line down to go through a bridleway gate, and descend down a field edge. At a disused pit, as our path drops alongside a fence, we are rewarded with a lovely view across an agricultural landscape to the **Solent** beyond, perhaps happy in the knowledge that we face no more steep hills! Passing through a bridleway gate, down a grassy track, we go through another gate, before crossing a road by a fingerpost (Wp.9 58M), then keeping ahead to turn left at the next road (Wp.10 62M). In 60m we turn right by a fingerpost on S19, a track. At the end of the left fence line, as the path opens out, we turn right (Wp.11 67M), passing down an arable field and over a stile to the right of a 'domed' copse. Maintaining direction, we cross a giant, prairie-like arable field, a novelty not to be constrained by fence or hedge. At the far side (Wp.12 73M), we turn left along the giant field edge, turning left again by a rusty steel post (Wp.13 79M), to cross the field and make for a plated steel post on the skyline ahead (Wp.14 81M). We bear half right, initially heading for a large distant stone barn, with the village of **Wellow** ahead, famous for the wind farm controversy. After another plated post, we descend, past a grain dryer and huge barn, to a road (Wp.15 88M). We turn right, and then left by a fingerpost, down an arable field edge and across the field to another road (Wp.16 90M). Crossing by the magnificent thatched farmhouse of **Rossiters Vineyard**, we pass the Post Office, ensconced in a long outbuilding, to a cinder track, then bear slightly right to pass through two vintage gates either side of the old railway line. The footpath threads through the vines, to go over a stile in the far corner, and diagonally crosses an arable field and another corner stile to a track (Wp.17 99M).

Turning right, rejoining the **Hamstead Trail**, a rising grassy track takes us onto a superbly surfaced permissive bridleway through a wood. Emerging by a gate, we bear right, passing a pair of isolated oak trees, and in 30m bear left to follow the right tree and hedge line, with a new plantation on our left. Passing through well separated trees, we go through a gate to turn right at the main road (Wp.18 110M)(bus stops nearby for an early return), and in 20m we cross, turning into **Hamstead Road**. The stony road takes us past an assortment of individual homes, and as the road swings left, we turn right by a fingerpost on S9 (Wp.19 117M), through a wood edge. Crossing a stile, we diagonally cross a meadow, going over two more, closely spaced, stiles. Maintaining direction, we cross the **Ningwood Lake** footbridge (Wp.20 123M), through a wood, leaving over a stile, and following the right fence line along a sizeable meadow. In the corner, we cross a final stile, turning right at the road to our destination, the **Horse and Groom** (Wp.21 130M), which is rapidly gaining a reputation for good food.

6. The Long Stone

Perhaps the most important ancient site on the Island, the **Long Stone** is part of a Neolithic long barrow complex, thought to have been a religious site used by Druids and Romans, and later as a meeting place by the Norse invaders.

From the old **Sun Inn** we make our way to **Hanover Point** on scenic paths, to join the **Coastal Path** along the beautiful cliff tops. Turning inland at **Chilton Chine** we pass **Mottistone Manor**, climbing through delightful bluebell woods to the **Long Stone**, returning on a wonderful path to the **Sun Inn**.

The coastal sections of this walk may be taken along the beach, tide permitting. Access points to the shore are at Waypoints 9, 10 and 13.

Access by bus: No.7 to the **Sun Inn**, **Hulverstone**
Access by car: Limited roadside parking east of the **Sun Inn**.

From the **Sun Inn** bus stop (Wp.1 0M), we walk past the pub, turning left onto a footpath by a fingerpost, and then following the left hedge line. Passing through a makeshift gate on the left (Wp.2 3M), we turn right to pass alongside a pond edge, before dropping down to loosely follow a very small stream, almost a ditch, down the meadow edge. Our path takes us over two stiles, then a third just after a stone cottage (Wp.3 13M), to bear right joining a track, which leads us into the scattered village of **Brook**.

At a road T-junction we turn left (Wp.4 16M), soon turning right opposite the unconventional village post office portacabin, into **Coastguard Lane** (Wp.5 17M). After passing a terrace of coastguard cottages, we continue ahead along a green lane, ignoring the fingerpost, with delightful views of **Freshwater Bay** ahead. Passing through a field gate, we follow the right fence line, with an attractive lake below on our left. After another field gate, we pass a stone cottage, onto a track (Wp.6 32M). Crossing a cattle grid, we follow an access track, bearing left, down to the **Military Road** (Wp.7 35M), then turning left along the verge before turning right (Wp.8 36M) crossing into the car park, with an ice cream van opportunity!

In the far right corner is an access path to the beach (Wp.9 37M), with its fossil forest and fascinating dinosaur footprints moulded in the sandstone, visible at spring low tides at **Hanover Point**.

The Coastal Path

We turn left to follow the impressive section of the **Coastal Path** along the cliff tops - the fossil bearing cliffs steadily being eroded by the sea, occasionally modifying our path as we progress. The path takes us inland around **Brook Chine** (Wp.10 50M, beach access), before turning back towards the sea, regaining the eastbound cliff path soon after a thatched stone cottage (Wp.11 53M). At a barbed wire fence we cross a stile (Wp.12 56M) to join the path on the sea side of the fence, negotiating cliff falls and slumps as they appear on this stunning route.

Approaching the white house of the **Isle of Wight Pearl**, we turn left at **Chilton Chine** (Wp.13 92M, beach access), passing through a small car park, and crossing the **Military Road** onto the access track to **Chilton Farm Cottages**. The track joins a tarmac road at the attractive cottages (Wp.14 99M), and we turn left along the winding **Hoxall Lane**. At a T-junction of roads (Wp.15 123M), we turn left, along the verge, crossing to pass in front of **Mottistone Manor**, with its fine gardens, and an optional visit to the nearby church.

Climbing the cutting

Spring Woodland

Small Copper Butterfly

on Mottistone Down

Just after the access road into the Manor, we climb a flight of wide steps (Wp.16 125M), turning right up BS43 footpath, with a spectacular display of bluebells in May, as we climb the cutting. At a fork of paths (Wp.17 130M) we keep right, through a stunning spring woodland with a spectacular display of bluebells in May, passing through a kissing gate and

The Long Stone

crossing a track to keep ahead. The **Long Stone** appears at the top, part of a Neolithic long barrow, the biggest standing stone on the island, and surrounded by myth and legend.

Passing the **Long Stone** (Wp.18 139M), we turn left, up a track, initially following the right fence line. Our track rises before continuing along the hillside of **Mottistone Common**, one of the Island's best paths, with spectacular views of the southwest coastline. (Look out for a smaller mystery standing stone away to the right.). Following the main winding track, ignoring all turn offs, we cross a stile into woodland, and turn left in 15m, on a lovely descending woodland path (Wp.19 153M). Emerging, we cross a meadow, go over a stile by a field gate, and loosely follow the left fence line to cross a stile in the left corner. A fence-enclosed path takes us through a kissing gate to emerge at the road opposite the 600 year old **Sun Inn** (Wp.1 162M).

7. Hamstead and the Tree Graveyard

A gentle walk from the **Horse and Groom** at **Ningwood**, passing the pretty **Ningwood Lake**, once navigable from the sea, but long silted up. We join the **Coastal Path** for most of the walk, with fine views across the beautiful, wildlife-rich, estuary of **Newtown River**. We make our way from **Hamstead Point** to **Yarmouth**, along the astonishing coastline, which is gradually sliding into the sea, as evidenced by the graveyard of trees lying on the beach, which is also rich in fossils. The sea-wall and promenade take us into **Yarmouth**, a town with a charm of its own, without excessive commercialism.

Short Walk: At Wp.5 keep ahead on footpath S27, keep left at a footpath junction on S30, turning left to rejoin the **Coastal Path** at the offset crossroads at Wp.11, near **Hamstead Farm**. (1 hour 50 mins, 4.6 miles/7.4km)

Access by bus: No.7 bus to the **Horse and Groom**, **Ningwood**.
Access by car: Roadside parking in **Station Road** opposite the **Horse and Groom**, bus back.

Newtown river jetty

Facing the **Horse and Groom** (Wp.1 0M), we turn right passing into the pub car park, turning left by a fingerpost along footpath S9 (Wp.2 1M), soon crossing a stile and turning left to follow the left hedge line of a large meadow. Crossing a stile in the corner, passing through a copse, we emerge to cross a footbridge over **Ningwood Lake** (Wp.3 9M). Turning right along the attractive bank, we cross a stile, our path passing through light, juvenile woodland and gorse. After crossing a plank bridge, and a stile, we turn right, then left by a marker post, following the left hedge line around a meadow and crossing a stile which appears on our left. An attractive, winding woodland path takes us over a plank bridge, and in 15m we turn right by a marker post on a path, which emerges at a wide track (Wp.4 15M), joining the **Coastal Path**. Turning left along the stone surfaced woodland track, we pass a three-way fingerpost before bearing right immediately after a cattle grid on S28 (Wp.5 21M). (For the short walk keep ahead on footpath S27).

The track eventually opens out with glimpses, through trees, of the beautiful, unspoilt **Newtown River** coming into view.

Passing **Lower Hamstead Farm** (Wp.6 39M), we continue ahead to the jetty, pausing to take in the spectacular views and abundance of birdlife on the salt marshes.

Boardwalk on the saltmarsh

Retracing our steps, we take the first right by a **Coastal Path** fingerpost (Wp.7 46M), onto a footpath, which emerges to skirt round a very attractive creek inlet and along a delightful boardwalk. At the head of the creek, our grass path bears left round the edge of a meadow, crossing stiles either side of the next meadow. We cross another superb boardwalk over a minor creek and along a woodland path. Turning a corner, we unexpectedly find ourselves at the top of steps descending to a shingle beach (Wp.8 63M), where we turn left along the top of the foreshore.

The fine grass path eventually veers away from the shoreline (Wp.9 68M), climbing into light woodland along the low cliff top, changing to a track flanked by fields and cliff edge woodland. Eventually we pass through **Hamstead Farm** (Wp.10 79M), following the winding farm track up to an offset crossroads, where we keep ahead, before climbing a stile next to a field gate by a **Coastal Path** fingerpost (Wp.11 83M).

Passing across a small meadow and over a stile, we bear half left, over a field, then along the left field edge, to pass through a field gate and along a narrow meadow. Crossing a stile we bear left on a grass path, forking right at a fingerpost (Wp.12 89M), still following the **Coastal Path**, along a field edge. After going through a copse, we cross a stile, to follow the right fence line across another field. Reaching a footpath gate, we continue ahead onto a track. At a track T-junction (Wp.13 93M) we turn left, keeping ahead at a crossroads of tracks on the **Coastal Path**, and in 45 metres turn right into

Tree Graveyard

West Close (Wp.14 97M). At the end, by a multi-way junction (Wp.15 99M), we turn sharp left by a fingerpost along a woodland path into **Bouldnor Forest**.

An occasionally muddy track leads us along the cliff top, with glimpses over the landmass gradually slipping into the sea. As if to prove the point, this fascinating path suddenly disappears into a 30m crater! We skirt round on the alternative path pioneered by fellow walkers, gradually descending through a pine wood to the seashore (Wp.16 124M), with its fantastic graveyard of trees strewn along the beach.

The beaches in this area are rich in fossils, about 28 million years old. Remains of turtles, crocodiles, fish, mammals and seeds can be found on the foreshore.

Passing through a reed-bed and along the top of the shore, we climb along the **Coastal Path** on a very winding

Winding woodland route

woodland route, regaining the beach with its further array of skeletal trees. The path veers away from the sea (Wp.17 129M), and we soon turn right onto a stony, rising access track, keeping ahead to the main road (Wp.18 136M). Crossing, we turn right, along the verge, crossing back to enter **Bouldnor Viewpoint** car park (Wp.19 141M). Keeping to the right side, we descend a path down to the sea wall, turning left along the top of the wall alongside the **Solent**, to eventually join the promenade. Turning left at the end, (Wp.20 151M), then right at the road, we keep ahead into **Yarmouth** - a pleasing town, with a good selection of interesting shops, pubs and eateries. We turn right (Wp.21 155M), passing the **Bugle Inn**, and then left past the **George Hotel** (nice garden), and the entrance to Henry VIII's castle. Crossing the road by the ferry loading ramp, we turn left along the harbour wall to the bus terminal (Wp.22 157M), to return whence we came.

8. Shalfleet, Winkle Street and Shorewell

From **Shalfleet**, a thriving port until the 17th century before silting ended trading, we follow the course of the **Caul Bourne** stream, passing **Calbourne Watermill Museum** and on to the village centre. We stroll down the very picturesque **Winkle Street**, before climbing over the forest clad **Brighstone Down**, emerging to enjoy marvellous views across the Channel coastline. From the summit of **Limerstone Down** we descend to the sleepy village of **Shorewell**, and the **Crown Inn**.

Short Walks:

(a) **Shalfleet** to **Calbourne**. Follow the route to the last cottage in **Winkle Street**. Turn right on a footpath, keeping ahead to the road. Turn right for the No.7 bus stop by the **Sun Inn**, **Calbourne**. (1 hour 5mins, 3.3 miles/5.3km)

(b) **Calbourne** to **Shorewell**. Take No.7 bus to the **Sun Inn**, **Calbourne**. At the crossroads, go downhill towards the church, starting the walk at Wp.12 opposite the well house. (1 hour 40mins, 4.7 miles/7.6km)

Access by Bus: No.7 to the **New Inn**, **Shalfleet**.
Access by Car: Turn up **Mill Road** alongside the **New Inn** to a car park, bus No.7 back.

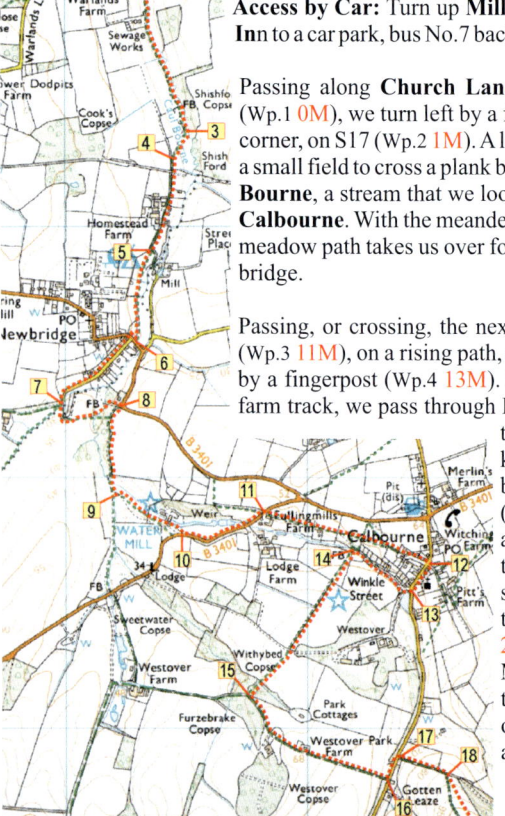

Passing along **Church Lane**, opposite the **New Inn** (Wp.1 0M), we turn left by a fingerpost, just around the corner, on S17 (Wp.2 1M). A left hedge line takes us into a small field to cross a plank bridge and stile by the **Caul Bourne**, a stream that we loosely follow all the way to **Calbourne**. With the meandering stream to our left, our meadow path takes us over four stiles and a double stile bridge.

Passing, or crossing, the next stile, we bear half right (Wp.3 11M), on a rising path, over a field to cross a stile by a fingerpost (Wp.4 13M). Bearing left along a wide farm track, we pass through **Homestead Farm**. As the track drops to our left, we keep ahead, crossing a stile by a fingerpost on S35 (Wp.5 17M). This attractive path, set along the hillside above the stream, takes us over a stile to turn right at a road (Wp.6 21M), on the outskirts of **Newbridge**. In 30m we turn left, along the length of **Clay Lane**, keeping left at the end by a fingerpost

waterside path

on S42 (Wp.7 28M). We soon turn left at a hedge gap by an electricity pole, initially following the left hedge line before veering right to cross a small field. We descend steps into a wetland wood, winding round to cross the **Caul Bourne** over a bridge, climbing steps onto a woodland path and turning right at a T-junction (Wp.8 32M).

This fabulous path snakes through the woods, descending to cross the stream over a charming footbridge and stile, where we turn left along the water's edge. We soon cross a plank bridge over the stream (Wp.9 36M) and along a beautiful small meadow. The path rises up another meadow to cross a stile into the car park of **Calbourne Water Mill**, emerging at the road (Wp.10 40M). Turning left we carefully follow the road, crossing the stream and turning right by a fingerpost up a flight of steps on CB13 (Wp.11

Winkle Street

45M). A series of stiles between paddocks takes us to a road, passing between cottages to a T-junction (Wp.12 56M), where we turn right opposite the village well house.

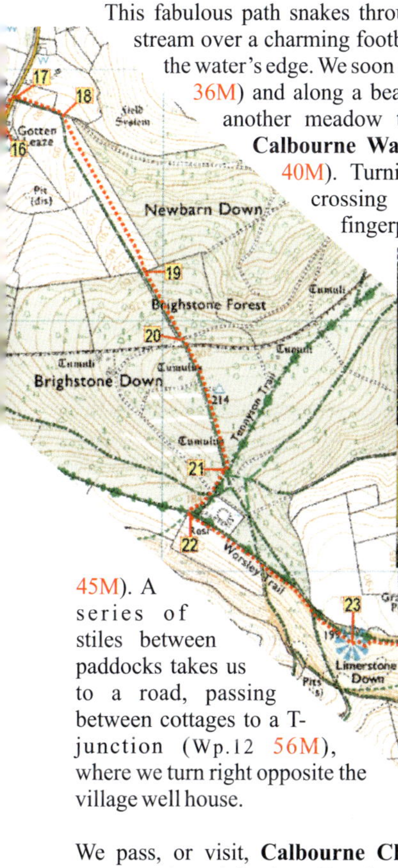

We pass, or visit, **Calbourne Church**, soon turning right into **Barrington Row** (Wp.13 58M). (More commonly known as **Winkle Street**, it is one of the prettiest locations on the Island, and unspoiled by commercial enterprises, although very busy in the holiday season.).

Having exercised our cameras, we follow the stream (for short walk (a) turn right after the last cottage). Crossing a stile and soon turning left over a footbridge (Wp.14 63M), we leave the **Caul Bourne** behind. We go over a series of four double stiles, crossing meadows, before dropping to cross a stile and footbridge into pretty woodland, **Withybed Copse**. We leave over another stile to turn left along a farm track (Wp.15 72M), with the heights of

Brighstone Forest stretching across the horizon ahead.

We make our way to a road (Wp.16 79M), turning left, then right at a parking area by a fingerpost up CB20 (Wp.17 80M), a rising track. At the top of a rise, we bear right through a field gate (Wp.18 83M), climbing up the middle of a

Limestone Down

very long, narrow, meadow to pass through a gate in the top right corner (Wp.19 93M). Taking a final backward glance at the **Solent**, we enter the Forest. The track climbs over a crossroads (Wp.20 97M), as we keep ahead across the summit of **Brighstone Down**.

The Channel coastline and **St Catherine's Down** come into view as we descend to a crossroads of tracks by a fingerpost, turning right on BS4 (Wp.21 107M). Emerging at a T-junction by a fingerpost (Wp.22 110M), we turn hard left, on a wide track, along the south edge of the forest. We climb to the summit of **Limerstone Down** (Wp.23 120M), with spectacular panoramic views to the southwest coast.

Descending towards Shorewell

Continuing east, alongside the main track, we gently descend across a wonderful downland landscape, passing a corrugated barn. The track kinks left, then right, through a double bridleway gate (Wp.24 131M), before we immediately bear right, passing through a nearby bridleway gate. Dropping down the hillside, we bear left, traversing a vague descending path. It is advisable to drop to follow the fence line below to the left, until the path to a bridleway gate appears. Passing through the gate (Wp.25 139M), we diagonally cross to the bottom left corner of a field, to go through another gate. We loosely follow the left fence line up and round to the left, turning right in the corner (Wp.26 146M) and pass through a nearby bridleway gate. Climbing over a hill, we descend across a meadow, bearing slightly right to seek a bridleway gate in the fence below, behind cottages. Passing through onto a path between the cottages, we emerge at a road (Wp.27 149M). Turning left, downhill, through the outskirts of **Shorewell**, we arrive at the **Crown Inn** (Wp.28 151M), and bus stops.

There can be few walks anywhere with such a selection of delightful paths. Words cannot do it justice. It has to be experienced!

Access by bus: No.7 to the **Three Bishops**, **Brighstone**.
Access by car: Village car park, down **Warnes Lane**, next to the **Three Bishops**.

From the **Three Bishops** (Wp.1 0M), we head down **Warnes Lane**, past a car park and playing field, to a road (Wp.2 2M). Turning right, we cross, and then turn left over a bridge crossing the **Buddle** stream. Passing along the left side of a playing field and then a hedge-lined path, we descend steps, crossing a road (Wp.3 5M) and up to the bridleway opposite. With distant downland views to the right and sea glimpses through the left hedge, we eventually pass through a bridleway gate to a road (Wp.4 16M).

Downland Views

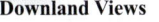

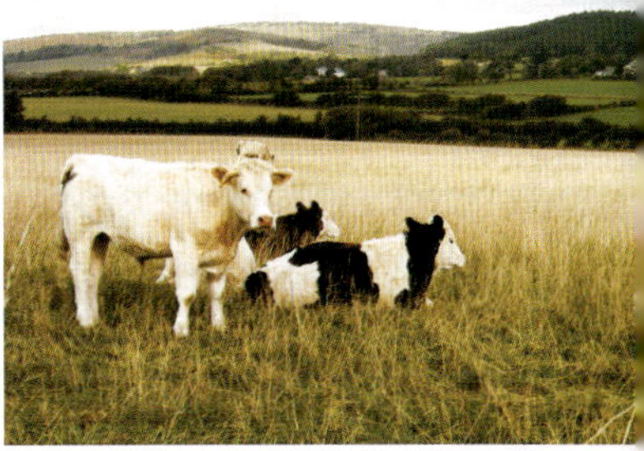

Turning left to the attractive **Chilton Farm Cottages**, we follow the road sharply round to the right (Wp.5 19M). Soon after a stone barn on our left, we turn right by a fingerpost on BS104 (Wp.6 21M), a very fine elm tree flanked path. At a T-junction with a road (Wp.7 31M), we turn right by an attractive cottage, climbing a slope and turning left by a fingerpost next to a house entrance, up BS67 (Wp.8 33M).

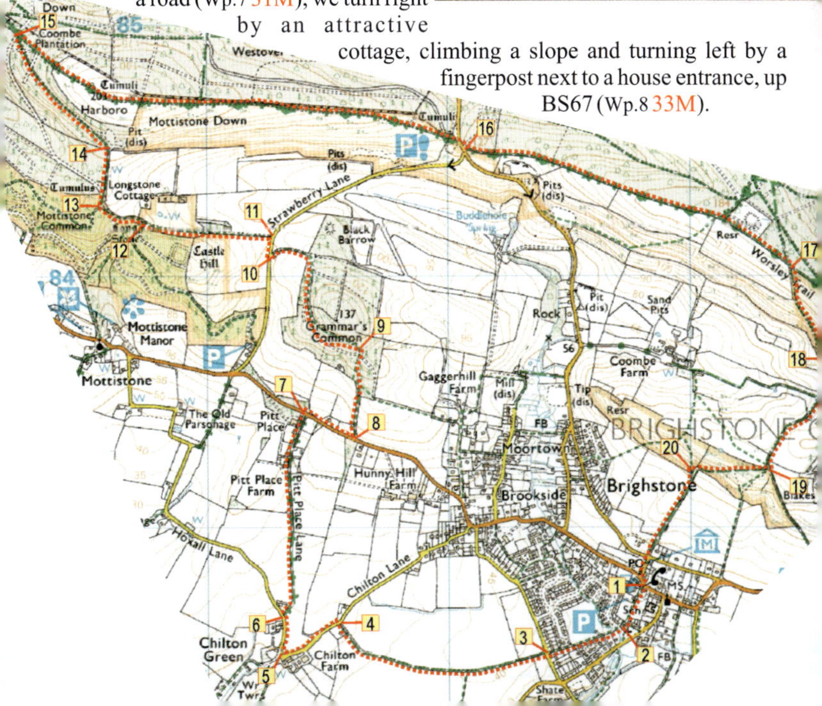

This path leads to the stunning **Grammars Common**, where we cross a stile into a beautiful mature pine wood on a soft carpet of pine needles. Turning left at a T-junction (Wp.9 38M), we continue climbing sharply before bearing left, flattening out along the flanks of the wooded hill. Emerging along a wide fern and gorse lined path, we eventually cross a stile, gently descending a track over a field and across another stile to a road (Wp.10 47M). Turning right, we rise to turn left at a fingerpost on BS84 (Wp.11 48M), entering the National Trust **Mottistone Estate**. Following the left hedge, we pass through a gate, soon emerging along an open field edge with the **Long Stone** ahead. The Neolithic long barrow is the biggest standing stone on the island, and is surrounded by myth and legend.

Passing the **Long Stone** (Wp.12 65M), we veer right up a rising track to a small clearing, and turn right to pass through a kissing gate (Wp.13 67M). A climbing woodland path takes us to emerge through a gate, bearing left up a beautiful grassy terraced path, BS88 (Wp.14 70M), with the most superb views across the coast to **Freshwater Bay** as we climb.

view across Freshwater Bay

the descending terraced path

North Street cottages

Our path gently drops through gorse to a T-junction with a track by two fingerposts (Wp.15 76M), where we turn hard right up the **Tennyson Trail**. Near the summit we pass several Bronze Age round barrows, with the option to visit, before passing through a gate onto **Mottistone Down** with fantastic coastal views. A descending path takes us by two more barrows, before passing through a gate and car park to a road (Wp.16 97M). Turning right, then immediately left up BS10, a wooded track which soon opens out, we climb steadily, utilising the right bank where possible.

Keeping ahead by an offset crossroads, we bear right at the next fingerpost crossroads (Wp.17 116M), through a bridleway gate, and down a fabulous descending grassy terraced path, with perfect views. Maintaining direction at a fingerpost (Wp.18 124M), we pass through a field gate, descending, and then rising, on a pleasing path. Cresting a rise, we bear right by a fingerpost on bridleway BS34 (Wp.19 130M) - yet another breathtaking path, dropping through bracken and gorse. Our sunken path steadily descends, bearing left (Wp.20 134M) between elm trees down impressive sandstone sided Sandy Lane. We go over a crossroads into **North Street**, passing the picturesque cottages, which house a National Trust shop and museum, with the thatched Post Office beyond. At the main road we turn left to return to the **Three Bishops** (Wp.1 139M), or **Brighstone Tea Rooms** by the church.

10. Newtown Nature Reserve.

The sacking of **Newtown** by the French in 1377 combined with the silting of the harbour to effect its demise as a flourishing Medieval town and seaport. The legacy, however, is a National Nature Reserve - a mecca for bird watchers, and a beautiful example of salt marsh habitat.

Our route meanders round the Reserve, visiting a remote bird hide and passing the **Old Town Hall**, before returning to the **New Inn**, **Shalfleet**.

2 | 1¾H | 5.4 miles/8.7km | 90m / 90m | 4

Access by bus: No.7 to the **New Inn**, **Shalfleet**.
Access by car: Turn up **Mill Road** alongside the **New Inn** to a car park.

From the traffic lights we turn into **Mill Lane**, passing the side of the **New Inn** (Wp.1 0M), and the free car park, before forking right (Wp.2 3M), downhill to pass **Shalfleet Mill**. A fine footbridge takes us over an attractive creek into woodland, before turning left by a marker post on a tarmac track. A left turn at a road T-junction (Wp.3 7M), takes us past a Scout camp entrance at a dip in the road, and we turn left through a kissing gate (Wp.4 9M) on a safe grass path paralleling the road along a meadow edge. After two more kissing gates we re-join the road, turning left down **Town Lane** (Wp.5 13M).

Having admired the very attractive **Fleetlands Farm**, we cross the picturesque causeway, turning left by a fingerpost (Wp.6 19M) on a footpath along the water's edge to cross a stile. Soon turning half right, uphill, we pass through a kissing gate, emerging at a road in **Newtown** (Wp.7 23M), and keeping ahead. At the road end (Wp.8 25M), we go through a kissing gate on footpath CB9, then pass through another gate, keeping left to follow the hedge line down to the stunning shoreline path of **Newtown** Nature Reserve through a kissing gate.

This delightful path leads us past a wooden boathouse by the quay (Wp.9

fabulous walkway bridge

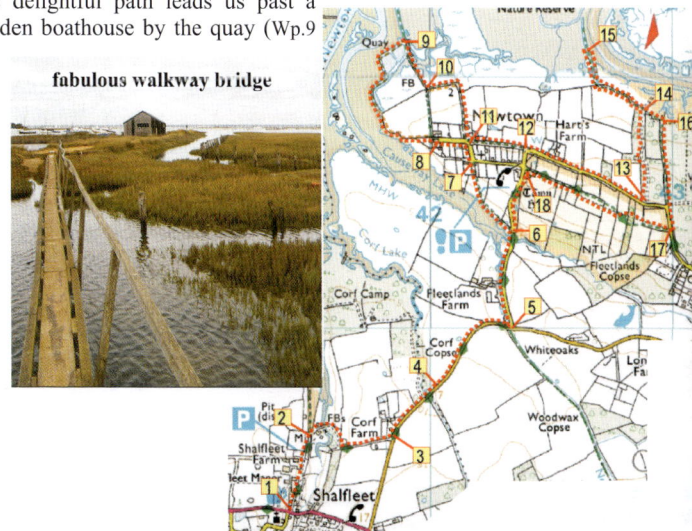

34M), before turning right to go over a fabulous walkway bridge across the salt marsh. At the end of the bridge, we turn left through a gate (Wp.10 38M), which takes us to the RSPB bird hide - well worth a visit and a check of the species board. Passing up the rising hedge-lined path toward **Newtown**, we turn left at the road (Wp.11 42M), and in 15m left again over a stile up a long, narrow, meadow. Crossing another stile (Wp.12 47M) we keep ahead along a road.

causeway to bird hide

As the road bends left, we turn left passing a wooden gate into **Town Copse** (Wp.13 52M), on a wide woodland track, which meanders through an active coppice. We eventually emerge to the salt marsh, turning left, just inside the trees on CB9 (Wp.14 55M), passing a hut. Crossing a stile, a meadow takes us to another stile where we turn right, along an eroding causeway, to visit a bird hide perched precariously on the end (Wp.15 61M).

a quiet spot

Retracing our steps to pass the hut by Wp.14, we keep ahead on a woodland path, just inside the trees, crossing a plank bridge. A left opening at a T-junction offers a quiet spot by the salt marsh (Wp.16 67M), as we turn right, entering a wood on a gently rising wide path. At a road we keep ahead, turning right in 90m by a fingerpost on CB13a and crossing a stile (Wp.17 72M). The grass footpath weaves through a series of small tree-lined meadows, loosely paralleling the nearby road, with an abundance of late summer fruits in the September hedgerows. Passing down a wide, hedge-lined path, we go through a kissing gate, turning left at a road (Wp.18 79M). We go by the historic **Old Town Hall** (c1699), dropping to cross the causeway bridge and retracing our outbound route to the **New Inn** (Wp.1 98M), which has a justified reputation for good food.

the old Town Hall

11. Newbridge, Shalfleet and Chessell Down

From the quiet village of **Newbridge**, we follow the course of the **Caul Bourne** stream to **Shalfleet**, with the **New Inn** and fine church. Crossing a farming landscape, we climb into the delightful **Brighstone Forest**, heading west over **Chessell Down**, and returning across prairie-like fields to **Newbridge**.

3 | 3H | 8.6 miles/13.8km | 250m / 250m | 4

Short Walks:
(a) **Shalfleet Loop**. Follow the route from Wp.1 to Wp.14, then turn left along **Clay Lane** to return to the start (1 hour 5 mins, 3.5 miles/5.6km).
(b) **Chessell Down Loop**. From the **Clay Lane** bus stop, **Newbridge**, walk up the hill and turn left along **Clay Lane** to start from Wp.14 (1 hour 55 mins, 5.4 miles/8.7km).

Access by bus: No.7 to **Clay Lane**, **Newbridge**. For an alternative start from the **New Inn**, **Shalfleet** - No.7 bus (start the walk from Wp.5).
Access by car: Roadside parking in **Clay Lane**, **Newbridge**. For an alternative start from the **New Inn**, **Shalfleet** - roadside parking in church lay-by or down **Mill Road** (start the walk from Wp.5).

From the **Clay Lane** (Newport bound) bus stop (Wp.1 0M), at the bottom of the hill, we cross the adjacent stile on S35. We follow the slightly elevated grass path along two narrow meadows, with **Caul Bourne** stream, the course of which we track to **Shalfleet**, below to our right. At the top left field corner, we cross a stile (Wp.2 4M), keeping ahead on an access road through **Homestead Farm** and over a stile by a fingerpost on S17. In 50m, we bear half right, crossing a stile (Wp.3 8M), diagonally descending a small meadow, then crossing or passing a stile in a gap in the trees below to loosely follow the course of the stream.

Our stream-side path passes through a series of meadows, crossing stiles and footbridges. Eventually, after passing a seat bench in the final meadow, we follow a right hedge line to a road (Wp.4 21M), turning right, around the church, to the **New Inn**, **Shalfleet** (Wp.5 22M).

We turn left, entering the churchyard through the main gate (Wp.6 23M), with the option to visit, before turning right and passing around the church tower, keeping ahead to drop down ancient stone steps to the road behind (Wp.7 24M). Turning right, then keeping right at the first T-junction, and left at the next (Wp.8 26M), we pass the Post Office, then a fine stone built farm, and leave the outskirts of the village. In 100m after the 'National Speed Limit' signs, we turn right on S15 by a fingerpost (Wp.9 31M), passing

stone steps behind church

bridge over Caul Bourne

through **Pondclose Copse**.

We emerge over a stile and turn half right across an arable field, making for a bridge stile by a gate in the hedge line. Crossing, we maintain direction to go over two closely spaced stiles in the far corner, turning left at a road (Wp.10 35M), then in 100m, right by a fingerpost on S16 (Wp.11 36M). A hedge-lined green lane takes us over a crossroads (Wp.12 47M), onto a rising road, past the attractive **Dodpits House**. As the slope levels out, we turn left by a fingerpost on S22 (Wp.13 53M), a farm access, with fine views to the forest-clad Downs, as we descend to pass through **Eades Farm**.

Keeping ahead to a track junction, we turn right by a finger post on S42 (Wp.14 59M), soon turning left at a hedge gap by an electricity pole, initially following the left hedge line before veering right to cross a small field. We descend steps into a wetland wood, winding round to cross the **Caul Bourne** over a bridge, climbing steps onto a woodland path and turning right at a T-junction (Wp.15 63M).

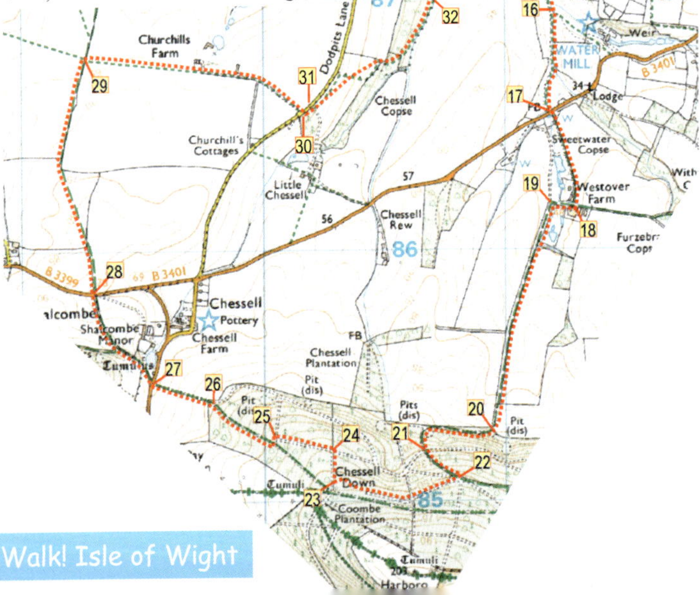

This fabulous path snakes through the woods, descending to cross the stream over a charming footbridge and stile, where we turn left along the water's edge, ignoring a sleeper bridge (Wp.16 75M) and keeping ahead. Following a stream tributary on our left, we pass through a long water meadow, **crossing a footbridge** stile in the far left corner. Carefully crossing a road, we go through a gate on CB16 (Wp.17 81M), passing a thatched cottage on a gently climbing track up to **Westover Farm** yard. We turn right in front of a large barn (Wp.18 86M) on a farm track, then cross a dip, before turning left on a wide stony track towards the Downs (Wp.19 87M). As the track swings right, we keep ahead up a wide green lane, to enter **Brighstone Forest** (Wp.20 100M), bearing right on a fine forest edge track.

As our track bends left, climbing steeply, we keep ahead crossing over another forest track (Wp.21 107M) up a narrower path, gradually curving left. Emerging at a T-junction (Wp.22 110M), we turn left, and immediately hard right up a gently rising path, traversing the slopes of **Chessell Down** between beech trees. As we progress, the path gradually narrows, until, at a T-junction with a track

climbing the forest track

(Wp.23 118M), we turn right, downhill. At a T-junction of paths (Wp.24 121M), we turn left on a level path, which then descends, suddenly turning sharp left for 15m to a T-junction (Wp.25 125M). We turn right, down a track, then left at a forest edge T-junction (Wp.26 127M), emerging through a gate before descending between fields to a road (Wp.27 129M).

Crossing, we go up an access track opposite, climbing and gradually curving right, before descending to pass through a gate and cross a road (Wp.28 134M). We follow the hedge line; pass through a bridleway gate, then diagonally cross a field to go through another gate in the far left corner to join a short path between fences.

After the confines of the forest we find ourselves crossing a vast open arable landscape with fine **Solent** views ahead. Following the right fence line to a rusty pole, we turn right, crossing a stile (Wp.29 147M), along a wide grass path between fields, surrounded by low panoramic views. We pass the secluded **Churchill Farm**, joining an access track to a road, where we turn left (Wp.30 157M). In 40m we turn right (Wp.31 158M), then immediately left, on S23, diagonally crossing the meadow to the bottom right corner. After a

cottage in Clay Lane

stile, a lovely woodland path levels and opens out, eventually going over a footbridge stile (Wp.32 165M), and crossing two meadow bottoms either side of a double stile bridge. We finally cross the last stile, (returning to Wp.14 169M), keeping ahead along the tarmac of **Clay Lane**, and passing several fine cottages as we enter **Newbridge**. We turn right at the end (Wp.33 173M) to return to the bus stop (Wp.1 174M).

12. Calbourne and Brighstone Forest

From the pretty village of **Calbourne**, we pass along 'chocolate box' pretty **Winkle Street** before crossing field and wood to enter **Brighstone Forest**. Passing through the forest, on wide meandering tracks, we leave to pass down a wonderful, peaceful isolated valley, rich in wildlife. Returning over the Downs via **Rowridge Farm**, and then passing near **Swainston Manor**, we cross an arable landscape for welcome refreshment at the **Sun Inn**.

Access by bus: No.7 to the **Sun Inn**, **Calbourne**.
Access by car: Roadside parking in **Lynch Lane**, opposite the **Sun Inn**, **Calbourne**.

We go down **Lynch Lane**, opposite the **Sun Inn** (Wp.1 0M), into the old village, going by the well house, and soon after the church turn right into **Barrington Row** (**Winkle Street**) (Wp.2 3M). Passing the picturesque waterside cottages, we continue on a footpath alongside the stream, crossing a stile (Wp.3 8M), and soon turning left to cross the stream over a footbridge. We go over a series of four double stiles, crossing meadows, before

Barrington Row

dropping to cross a stile and footbridge into attractive woodland, **Withybed Copse**.

Emerging over a stile to a track T-junction (Wp.4 16M), we turn right, passing through the farmyard of **Westover Farm**, crossing a dip, and turning left up a stony track (Wp.5 21M) towards the heights of **Brighstone Forest**. As the track swings right, we keep ahead, up a wide green way, entering the forest (Wp.6 35M) and bearing right on a wide path just inside the forest edge. The path curves left, climbing steeply. We keep ahead over a track crossroads (Wp.7 41M), before gradually veering left on a rising narrow woodland path. At a T-junction (Wp.8 44M), we turn left on the slightly rising main track to a major spacious crossroads (Wp.9 48M). We turn left again, on the main chalky track, gently meandering down through the forest.

At **Calbourne Bottom**, going through a bridleway gate (Wp.10 64M), we bear right, crossing the road to pass through another gate by a fingerpost on BS9. We keep to the right fork (Wp.11 65M), initially paralleling the road before

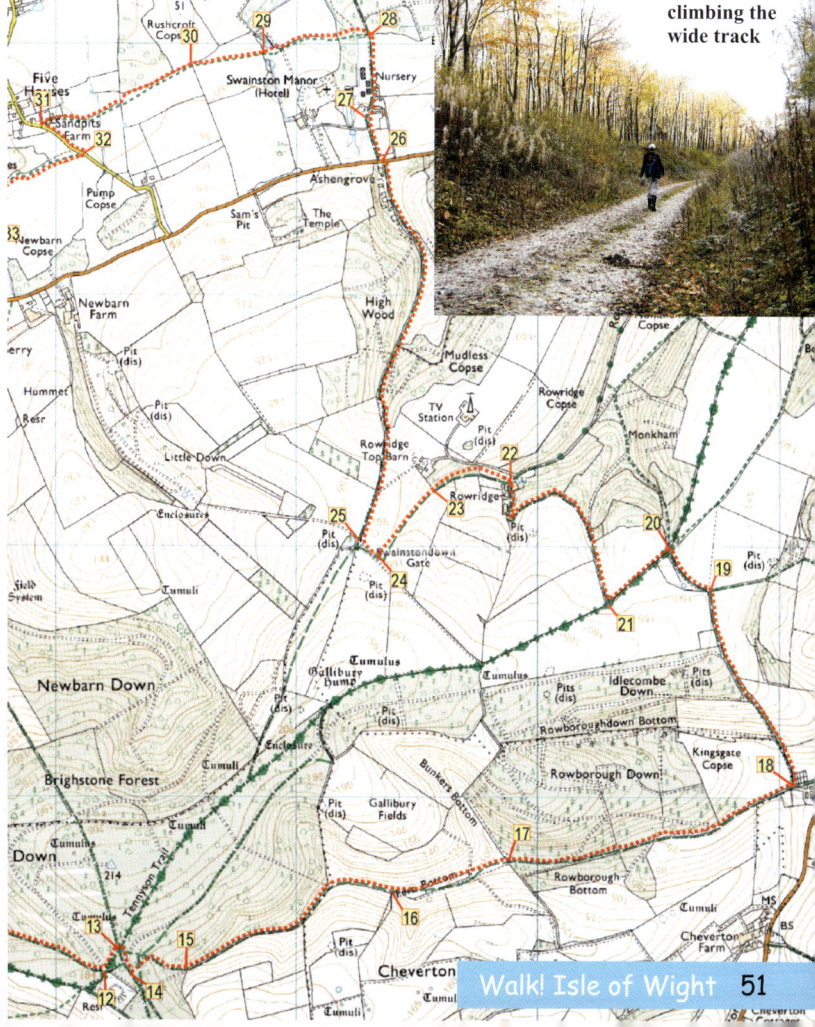

climbing the wide track

curving left for a steady forest climb up a shallow valley bottom, on a wide airy track.

At the top, by a fingerpost, we turn left on BS4 (Wp.12 81M), then hard right in

storm clouds over the valley junction

100m by a fingerpost (Wp.13 83M). In 60m we keep ahead over a fingerpost crossroads, turning left in 35m at a fingerpost T-junction on BS7 (Wp.14 85M), a descending path through sweet chestnuts. We meander down, to leave through a bridleway gate (Wp.15 89M) and turn left to loosely follow the forest fence down a meadow edge.

Fern Bottom

This stunning isolated valley, one of the quietest spots on the Island, takes us through a field gate, descending to a beautiful open valley junction and down **Fern Bottom** - haunt of spiralling buzzards. We follow the valley down, passing through a bridleway gate (Wp.16 99M), and keep left to follow the right fence line, making for a bridleway gate in a crossing fence at the right side of the valley bottom (Wp.17 108M). Going through, we re-enter the forest along **Rowborough Bottom**, a peaceful, semi-open woodland. We pass through several bridleway gates on our gentle descent, before emerging on a valley bottom track between fields.

Passing through another gate, down a chalky track, we turn left at a T-junction, just after going under power lines (Wp.18 125M). A strenuous climb up a flinty track, with increasingly fine views opening out, takes us over the top. We follow the main track left (Wp.19 138M) descending to go through a bridleway gate by a field gate, and on to a nearby 5-way junction by a fingerpost (Wp.20 142M). We turn hard left, uphill, soon passing through a field gate and up the edge of an arable field to a fingerpost T-junction, where we turn right down N198 (Wp.21

Christmas Dinner?

146M). Passing through a bridleway gate, we follow the left fence down a meadow edge, through a field gate onto a farm track. We wind down to pass through the middle of **Rowridge Farm**, perhaps greeted by a cacophony of turkeys!

We turn left in front of the farmhouse (Wp.22 155M) through a field gate, across a grass enclosure and through a bridleway gate. Ascending a lovely path along a coppice edge, we emerge through a field gate (Wp.23 160M), keeping ahead to climb a shallow valley up a field to a fingerpost, silhouetted on the skyline (Wp.24 168M). Turning right on a farm track, we soon turn left before a nearby fingerpost, through a temporary gate (Wp.25 169M), and immediately turn right through a bridleway gate, to pass the previously identified fingerpost, as we descend on CB21, following the right fence line down a meadow.

Making the most of fine **Solent** views, before going through a gate in the field corner, we descend a tree-lined track. We pass through a narrow clearing, and follow a wood edge down past the hamlet of **Ashengrove** to the main road (Wp.26 187M). Crossing, we go down a concrete road signed '**Swainston Manor**', which forks right (Wp.27 190M), passing a cottage, and at a fingerpost we turn left on a footpath (Wp.28 194M) to wend through a wood. The pleasing path emerges over a footbridge and stile, following the right hedge line along an arable field, with **Swainston Manor** opposite. Crossing a farm track, by a pond (Wp.29 200M), we diagonally cross an arable field to the far right corner, passing through a hedge gap by a marker post (Wp.30 204M), and now following the right hedge line. Crossing a stile near the corner, still following the weaving right hedge, we pass to the left of a barn, and over another stile to turn left at a road (Wp.31 216M), near the attractive **Sandpits Farmhouse**.

We turn hard right by a fingerpost, crossing a stile on CB10 (Wp.32 218M), before threading our way through a disused pit, and rising to follow the convoluted right fence line of a large arable field. Eventually we turn right (Wp.33 225M), crossing three closely spaced footbridges, to proceed along a fence-enclosed path, dropping down steps to a road (Wp.34 229M), where we turn left to return to the **Sun Inn** (Wp.1 233M).

13. Brighstone Bay

The centre of **Brighstone** retains its olde worlde village charm, with its pub, church, tea room, local shops and delightful local museum. Our route takes us across rich farmland to pass through **Yafford**, over **Samber Hill**, to **Shepherd's Chine** and along the fabulous **Brighstone Bay** cliff top path. We return up **Marsh Chine**, on paths that take us right into the village centre, for welcome refreshments at tea room or pub.

Access by bus: No.7 to **Brighstone**, **Three Bishops** pub.
Access by car: Park in **Brighstone** village car park in **Warnes Lane** next to the **Three Bishops**.

Facing the **Three Bishops** pub (Wp.1 0M), we turn left, passing **Brighstone Tea Rooms** and entering the churchyard to pass around the Victorian embellished church. Re-joining the road, we pass a thatched cottage on the left before turning right down **Broad Lane**, immediately crossing a stile on the left (Wp.2 3M) and following a right fence line down a field. When researched, the bottom of the field was waterlogged –a hindrance overcome by ignoring two stiles and keeping left to skirt round the boggy part to re-gain the footpath on the lower edge of the field before crossing a stile in the corner (Wp.3 9M).

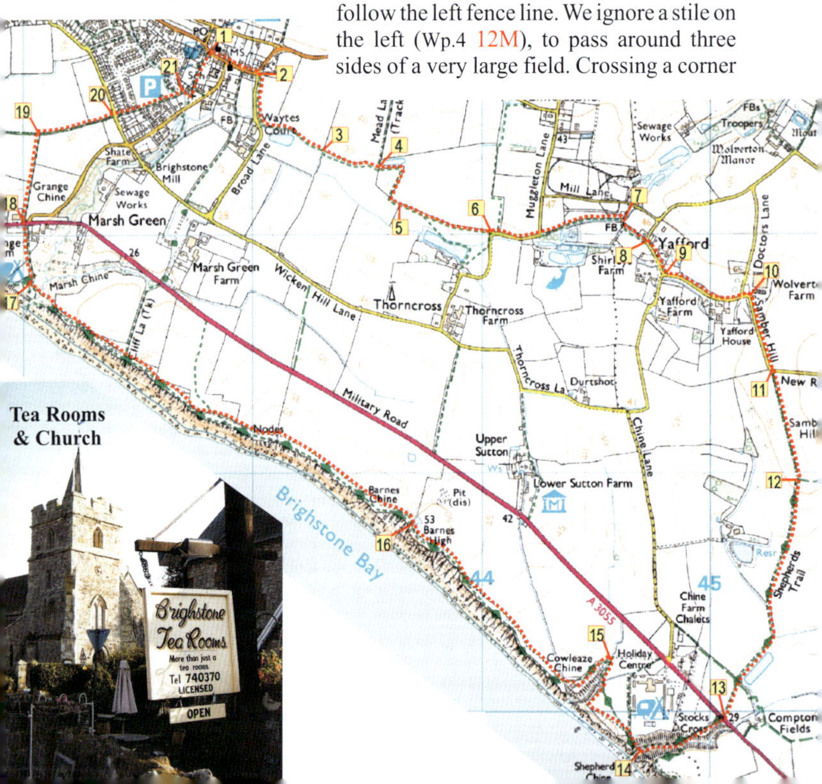

Now following a right hedge line, we cross a double stile in the next corner, to follow the left fence line. We ignore a stile on the left (Wp.4 12M), to pass around three sides of a very large field. Crossing a corner stile and plank bridge (Wp.5 17M), we follow the left reed-lined ditch on a slightly raised path. Going over another stile with bridge, we join a country lane, keeping ahead (Wp.6 23M). As the lane bears sharply left, we maintain direction on footpath BS105, crossing a stile with pleasing distant downland views away to the left. Turning right over a footbridge (Wp.7 29M), then bearing left over a nearby stile, we pass along a field edge, crossing another stile into a lane (Wp.8 31M). Turning right, we go through the scattered hamlet of **Yafford**, to turn left by an attractive pond (Wp.9 33M), up **Mill Lane**.

Passing the fine **Yafford House**, we keep ahead at **Doctors Lane**, soon bearing right up the gently climbing hill (Wp.10 38M). As our lane bears left, we continue ahead by a fingerpost (Wp.11 42M), on bridleway SW22, up **Samber Hill**, with downland and coastal views opening out. At a fingerpost we join the **Shepherd's Trail** on SW22a (Wp.12 47M), keeping ahead and passing over a wide agricultural landscape, to cross the **Military Road** onto footpath SW25 by a fingerpost (Wp.13 60M).

keeping 'ahead' at the fingerpost

With the deep **Shepherd's Chine** on our left, passing along the right side of a small meadow, we descend a track, joining the **Coastal Path**, and keeping along the right side of the Chine on an adventurous, weaving route. At the top of a flight of beach access steps (Wp.14 66M), we turn right, climbing sharply, following the **Coastal Path** along the tops of the fossil-rich, eroding cliffs. Our route passes round **Cowleaze Chine** (Wp.15 72M), via a camp site, to regain the cliff, with the occasional alarming crack across our path. With stunning views along the coast to the towering chalk cliffs of **Tennyson Down**, startling displays of thrift in June, and the murmur of the sea below, we go over **Barnes High** (Wp.16 91M), eventually dropping down a flight of steps into **Marsh Chine**.

looking back from Barnes High

Crossing a fine wooden footbridge, we climb to a track, passing through a small caravan park, and turning right up a steep tarmac access (Wp.17 115M), which returns us to the **Military Road**. Crossing, we go over a stile by a fingerpost opposite (Wp.18 119M), passing up the right side of a narrow meadow. After a double stile bridge, we continue up the right side of a large arable field to climb another stile (Wp.19 123M), turning right, along bridleway BS62. We cross a road (Wp.20 127M), and climb concrete steps, to join a shady footpath BS24 before keeping right through a playing field to cross a bridge over the **Buddle** stream. We turn right (Wp.21 131M), cross the road, and then turn left by a fingerpost on BS25. The tarmac path takes us past a car park to join a lane, which almost unexpectedly emerges in the village centre by the **Three Bishops** pub (Wp.1 133M).

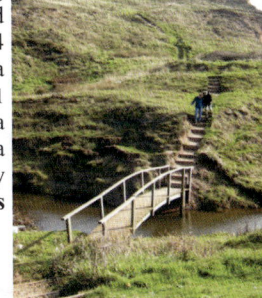
Marsh Chine footbridge

14. Gallibury Hump and Bowcombe Down.

From the **Blacksmiths Arms**, we take a farmland route, passing a fine farmhouse, with a brief interlude along the old railway line to **Yarmouth** before a steady climb through wood and field into **Brighstone Forest**. Passing a most impressive round barrow, **Gallibury Hump**, we descend to a delightful valley and shady track to the hamlet of **Bowcombe**, before climbing the Down to enjoy the **Solent** view, returning to the **Blacksmiths Arms**, locally known as the "Betty 'aunt", after a local folk tale.

| 3 | 2½H | 7.4 miles/11.9km | 280m / 280m | ↻ | 3 |

Access by bus: No.7 on the **Calbourne Road**, the **Blacksmiths Arms**.

Blacksmith's Arms

Access by car: Blacksmiths Arms car park with prior permission.

Facing the **Blacksmiths Arms** (Wp.1 0M), we turn right, carefully along the road, to the top of a rise, turning left over a stile by a fingerpost (Wp.2 2M). We descend down the middle of a large meadow, crossing a stile and turning right down a farm track, soon bearing left to a crossroads (Wp.3 7M).

Turning left, up a rising track, we pass through a gate by a farm, keeping ahead along a gently rising access track to cross a road, **Betty Haunt Lane** (Wp.4 12M).

Betty, a smuggler's daughter, was adept at distracting the Excise men with her feminine charms, whenever contraband was due! Unfortunately for her, she fell in love with an Excise officer and betrayed her smuggler friends. Some were caught, but some escaped, to wreak their revenge by strangling Betty. Her ghost may still haunt the Lane!

Great Park Farm

We soon pass a delightful pair of brick built farm cottages on the access road, which takes us past the impressive **Great Park Farm**. Keeping ahead, we descend from the farm to join the old railway line, with a lovely southerly aspect. At a fingerpost by a junction of tracks, we fork left by what was **Watchingwell Halt** station (Wp.5 29M), on a stony track, then keeping ahead at a fingerpost T-junction on CB25 (Wp.6 32M). The track initially curves left, before winding to a T-junction (Wp.7 35M), where we turn left on a wooded track, passing near the almost hidden **Swainston Manor**, eventually emerging to cross the main **Calbourne Road** (Wp.8 42M).

We pass up **Ashengrove Farm** access road, soon keeping to the left of a hedge on a steadily rising track. Passing a corrugated barn, we keep right, up the edge of a wood, on a wide track, climbing up through woodland with an abundance of pheasants. Emerging through a field gate, we follow the left hedge line, with wide ranging Island views opening out as we ascend. Passing a fingerpost, we go through a bridleway gate on BS6 (Wp.9 64M), rising up the right side of a very large field on an invisible path to loosely follow the right fence line. As the field starts to funnel

Gallibury Hump

in, we go through a bridleway gate on the right (Wp.10 74M), maintaining direction up a hedge-lined track and entering the stunning eastern end of **Brighstone Forest**. We turn hard left at a T-junction (Wp.11 79M), on a well-surfaced forest track, which opens out with **Gallibury Hump** in a field to our left. The **Hump** is probably the biggest round barrow on the Island. Folklore has it that it was once the site of a gallows.

Soon after passing a fingerpost junction, we go through a field gate, keeping ahead along a field edge, and starting our descent, with long views over the northeast and **Portsmouth** beyond. Going through a bridleway gate, on N136a (Wp.12 93M), the track bears left, revealing the southeast coast. We keep ahead, passing a fingerpost junction, before going through a field gate, dropping to a five-way fingerpost junction and passing through a bridleway gate (Wp.13 103M). Bearing slightly right, we follow the right fence line up a

the shady track

view to the Solent

large field, and then descend to cross a stile. We continue down the right side of a pasture descending into a lovely valley, passing through two field gates and bearing right by a fingerpost (Wp.14 118M). A delightful shady track gently descends to a road (Wp.15 130M), where we turn left along the footway at the hamlet of **Bowcombe**.

Opposite **Whitelane Farm**, at the top of a rise, we turn left (Wp.16 132M), by a fingerpost on N127, up a track. Keeping right, we go through a field gate, up a sunken enclosed track to climb **Bowcombe Down**. Towards the top, we go through a gate, keeping ahead and crossing a multi-way junction (Wp.17 143M) on a still rising track. As we crest the brow of the **Down**, we are amply rewarded by a lovely view across **Newtown Creek** and the **Solent** beyond. The track descends to return us to the **Blacksmiths Arms** and bus stops (Wp.1 154M).

15. Thorness Bay

Apart from several short sections on quiet roads, this walk is entirely on footpaths, along meadow, woodland and farm track, passing the **Sportsman's Rest** at **Porchfield** and down a beautiful path to the beach. A unique, adventurous, low tide foreshore walk, with its fascinating geology, takes us to **Thorness Bay** before turning inland to return. This walk should only be undertaken two hours either side of low tide.

Access by bus: No.30 to **Hillis Corner** (Southern Vectis and Wightbus)
Access by car: Alternative start from the **Sportsman's Rest**, **Porchfield**, commencing at Wp.5.

From the **Hillis Corner** mini-roundabout (Wp.1 0M), we take the **Thorness** road, bearing right at a road junction up **Rolls Hill** (Wp.2 1M). After passing a copse on the left, we turn left, crossing a stile by a fingerpost (Wp.3 8M), on CB4, then maintaining direction along the edge of **Chalkclose Copse** over meadows, through a small copse and crossing stiles between. We go over a stile near a house by a fingerpost, turning right (Wp.4 17M), and passing through a field gate on a descending track. After another gate, we go up into **Stagwell Farm**, bearing right then left at the farmhouse (Wp.5 21M) on a short stretch of fenced path to go over a stile. Crossing a small meadow and a corner stile, we keep ahead across a meadow and footbridge stile, and then bear left to very loosely follow the left hedge line to cross a stile in the far left corner (Wp.6 26M), entering the north west corner of **P a r k h u r s t Forest**.

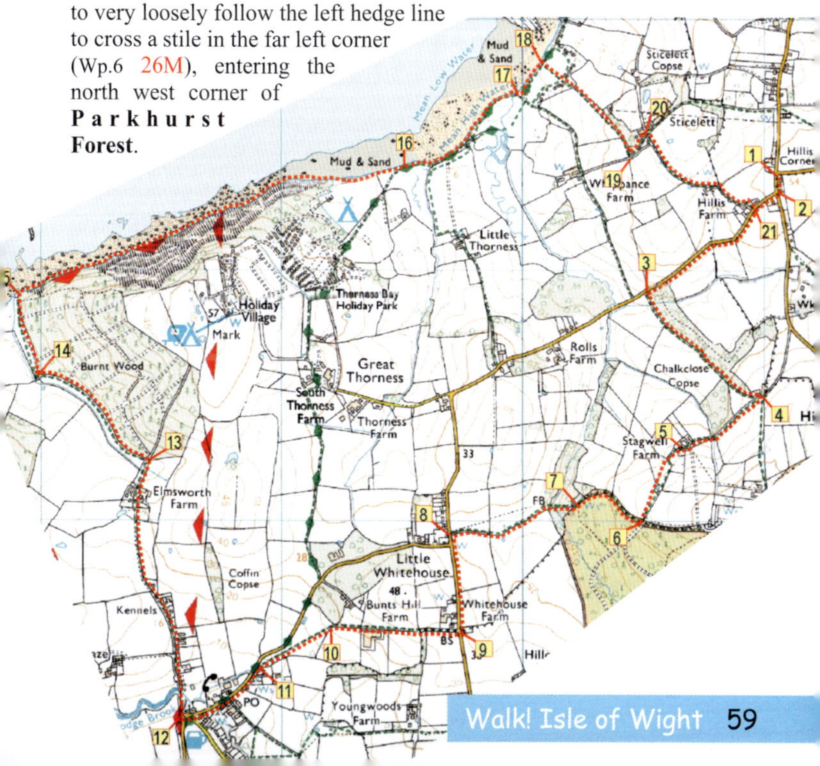

We soon turn hard right, at a path crossroads, initially descending just inside the forest edge, and then winding through the fine deciduous woodland. Keeping ahead by a stile (Wp.7 30M), we cross a footbridge and stile into a meadow, loosely following the left hedge line, and crossing two further stiles to emerge at a road (Wp.8 36M). Turning left, we maintain direction at a nearby road junction, passing **Whitehouse Farm** near the top of a slope, and turn right by a fingerpost on CB11a (Wp.9 40M), a wide grass track. Crossing a stile, we loosely follow the left hedge over two meadows with stile between, enjoying fine low westerly views. We go over, or round, the next stile (Wp.10 45M), turning half left down an odd-shaped meadow to cross another stile in the far right corner (Wp.11 48M), bearing left along a road into the village of **Porchfield**.

Elmsworth farmhouse

Passing the recommended **Sportsman's Rest** pub, we turn right at the War Memorial (Wp.12 56M), down **Elmsworth Lane**. The road crosses **Rodge Brook**, eventually becoming a stony track by a cottage, with pleasant views over **Newtown Creek**. Passing the attractive **Elmsworth Farmhouse**, and through the working farmyard, we turn left before a field gate at the wood edge ahead, crossing a stile (Wp.13 68M). A beautiful path meanders down delightful narrow meadows alongside **Burnt Wood**. Crossing a stile (Wp.14 76M), we bear right, go over another stile (Wp.15 80M),

looking back from the stile

Firing Range sign

just before I slipped!

and turn right again to walk along the lovely isolated stretch of beach.

Extreme care should be taken. Avoid flat clay surfaces (slippery as ice). Keep to the shingle wherever possible, and clamber with care over the corpses of trees, where necessary. This coastline is gradually sliding into the sea on a layer of blue slipper clay lubricated by rainfall. Where a landslip occurs across the beach, the surface becomes very soft. Light rapid steps should take you over without getting that sinking feeling! The fascinating geology is evident in the low clay faced cliffs, where bands of fossilised shells can be seen - about 30 million years old!

Opening out at **Thorness Bay**, where geese, ducks and waders are often present, we pass along the top of the beach, with the **Coastal Path** joining us (Wp.16 98M). Crossing a concrete bridge (Wp.17 115M), we turn left by a fingerpost, to continue along the rear of the beach. A stile appears at the top of the right bank. We climb, to cross it (Wp.18 117M), and follow the left fence line up a meadow, away from the sea. Over a stile, we pass between fences, then cross another stile to pass up the left side of two meadows, with a bridge stile between, turning left in the top left corner over a final stile bridge (Wp.19 125M), and through a narrow copse. Emerging to join a concrete access road, we turn right at a T-junction by a fingerpost (Wp.20 127M), following the farm access with fine westerly views. We meander back to the road (Wp.21 133M), turning left to retrace our outward route back to the **Hillis Corner** mini-roundabout (Wp.1 136M).

looking back across Thorness Bay

16. Parkhurst Forest

The Island is fortunate in its abundance of woodlands, with the 1,100 acres of **Parkhurst Forest** being a mix of ancient woodland and plantation. The forest, classed as a Site of Special Scientific Interest, is rich in wildlife, including red squirrel, nightjar, and long eared owl.

From the **Blacksmiths Arms**, on the **Calbourne Road**, an agricultural walk takes us into the forest, visiting the red squirrel hide, and across a delightful semi-open area in the heart of the forest. A series of footpaths with plenty of stiles, takes us to **Porchfield** and the **Sportsman's Rest** before returning over meadows and along an old railway line.

Short Walk: Follow the route to Wp.29 at **Lower Watchingwell**, return on bus No.7 (Shalfleet route) (2hours 15mins, 7.4 miles/11.9km).

Access by bus: No.7 to the **Blacksmiths Arms** (Calbourne route).
Access by car: Blacksmiths Arms car park with prior permission, or an alternative start from the **Sportsman's Rest**, **Porchfield** (start at Wp.24).

Facing the pub (Wp.1 0M), we turn right, carefully negotiating the busy road to the top of a rise and turning left over a stile by a fingerpost on N73 (Wp.2 2M). We descend down the middle of a pasture, crossing a stile, and turning right on a farm track, which turns left down to a track crossroads above **Reads Farm** (Wp.3 7M). We turn right, soon turning left through a gate, and immediately right along a rising access road. As the road bends right, we keep ahead over a stile, along the bottom edge of an arable field onto a farm track, passing behind **Alvington Manor Farm**.

Opposite the last barn (Wp.4 21M), we fork left on a descending farm track, with **Parkhurst Forest** ahead, to cross the course of the old railway line.

entering the forest

Keeping ahead, we cross a stile at the bottom left corner of a meadow, then bear left over a plank bridge stile (Wp.5 26M) to loosely follow the left hedge across an arable field to a road junction (Wp.6 29M). We turn right, down a concrete access, to cross the main road (Wp.7 38M), and enter the 1,100 acre forest up a wide gravel track.

Turning right on another wide gravel track (Wp.8 40M), we fork left in 70m (Wp.9 41M), up a grassy, rising track, ignoring crossing paths, and keeping ahead at a crossroads by a giant fingerpost (Wp.10 49M). We head for the red squirrel viewing hide, claimed to be 100m away but actually over 200m. We turn left by a carved squirrel

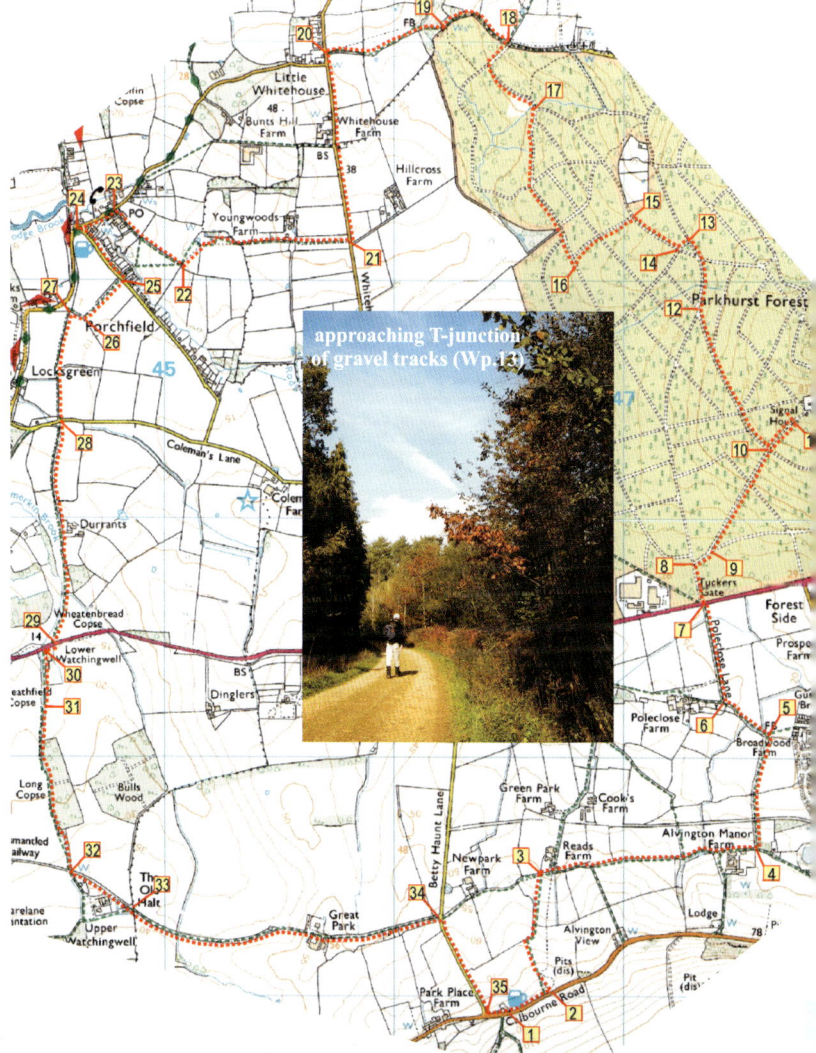

the red squirrel hide

(Wp.11 51M), to visit the hide, hoping for a sighting of this shy creature.

Re-tracing our steps to the giant fingerpost, we turn right at the crossroads, along a stony forest track, again ignoring all crossing paths. As a gravel track joins from the left (Wp.12 62M), we continue ahead to a T-junction of gravel tracks (Wp.13 67M), turning left, and in 50m, right (Wp.14 68M), on a gently rising grassy track, which gradually narrows to a path. At a fork of paths (Wp.15 71M), we bear left, crossing a fabulous semi-open area along a winding path, deep in the forest. Eventually we turn right, downhill, at a T-junction by a new plantation (Wp.16 77M), keeping ahead as we join a gravel track. At the next T-junction (Wp.17 84M), we turn left on a narrower gravel path, soon rising and bearing right before passing through a carved timber arch (Wp.18 91M).

approaching T-junction of gravel tracks (Wp.13)

carved timber arch Wp.18

We turn left on a lovely woodland path, initially just inside the forest edge, then undulating through the trees. Passing a stile (Wp.19 95M), we keep ahead to cross a footbridge and stile beyond, emerging into a meadow, then loosely following the left hedge line over two more stiles to a road (Wp.20 100M). Turning left and keeping ahead at a nearby junction, we gently climb to pass **Whitehouse Farm**, with fine low views to the west of the Island, as we crest the brow of a hill.

Descending a long straight, we turn right by a fingerpost on N150 (Wp.21 112M), the access to **Youngwoods Farm**. Maintaining direction, we cross a stile, passing in front of the attractive farmhouse, and follow the right hedge line across two meadows and two stiles, keeping ahead over the next meadow to cross another stile (Wp.22 121M). Bearing right, to again follow the right hedge line of a meadow, we cross a stile and a small meadow, then pass through a footpath gate and a fine working farmyard going through a gate to turn left at a road (Wp.23 129M).

Passing the recommended **Sportsman's Rest Inn**, we turn left along **New Road** (Wp.24 131M), then right over a stile by a fingerpost on CB7 (Wp.25

Sportsman's Rest (recommended)

135M), to the far right corner of a meadow. We turn right over a stile (Wp.26 138M), then cross another, nearby, immediately turning left over a third by a fingerpost (Wp.27 139M). Following the left hedge line, we pass along two meadows with a gate between, crossing a stile onto an enclosed path and emerging to cross a road by a fingerpost (Wp.28 145M).

We soon cross a stile into a meadow, following the left hedge, crossing a track, and continuing ahead to pass a rusty fingerpost in the next field. As the left hedge veers left, we descend diagonally to pass through a field gate in the far right corner, now following the right hedge to cross a stile onto the main road at **Lower Watchingwell** (Wp.29 157M). (Short walk option of the No.7 bus from the nearby bus stops to the left).

We turn right, and in 35m left, crossing the road (Wp.30 158M) onto an access track by a small barn, and soon passing a farmhouse onto a grassy path twixt hedges. Following the right hedge of a large arable field, and crossing through a substantial gap to swap sides (Wp.31 162M), we now follow the left side of the hedge. By a fingerpost, we turn left (Wp.32 173M), along the wide course of the old railway line, past the old **Watchingwell Halt** station - now a house (Wp.33 177M), just before a bridleway track joins from the right by a fingerpost.

Maintaining direction on N149, we eventually leave the trackbed to climb past the imposing **Great Park Farmhouse**, and on to a crossroads with **Betty Haunt Lane** (Wp.34 188M) (see page Walk 14 for the story). We turn right, up the lane, turning left at the top (Wp.35 193M) to return to the **Blacksmiths Arms** (Wp.1 194M).

17. Porchfield, Gurnard and Cowes

A fine walk at any time of year, but without a doubt, the best time for this walk is during Cowes week, when **West Cowes** comes alive during the most famous regatta in the world.

drama on the Solent

From **Lower Watchingwell**, we cross stile and meadow to **Porchfield**, with the notable **Sportsman's Rest** pub. We follow the **Coastal Path** around the lovely crumbling coastline of **Thorness Bay** to pass through **Gurnard** and along a wonderful series of seafront promenades, taking us into the fascinating yachting mecca of **West Cowes**. A trip over the **River Medina**, on the quirky chain ferry, takes us to our final destination at **East Cowes**.

3 | 2¾ H | 7.9 miles/12.7km | 125m 145m | 3

Access by bus: No.7 on the **Shalfleet** route to **Upper Watchingwell Bridleway** bus stop. Return on No.4 or 5 from **East Cowes** Town Hall
Access by car: Park near **East Cowes** Town Hall, bus No.5 to **Newport**, then No.7 to **Upper Watchingwell Bridleway**, walk back.

From the **Yarmouth** bound bus stop (Wp1 0M), we head west, towards **Shalfleet**, and in 90m turn right over a stile by a fingerpost on CB8 (Wp.2 1M). Loosely following **Clamerkin Brook** hidden on our left, we pass through a field gate, then along two narrow meadows, crossing stiles in the far right corners of both. Keeping ahead, we cross a nearby road onto a footpath opposite (Wp.3 9M), passing through a narrow copse and crossing a plank bridge stile. Bearing right, we follow the right hedge line of a meadow, maintaining direction as we pass through a field gate to the left of the far right corner. Another right hedge line and corner stile, take us to a T-junction with a farm track (Wp.4 17M). Turning left, crossing a stile at the nearby road (Wp.5 18M), we turn right towards **Porchfield** village, bearing right at a small War Memorial (Wp.6 22M).
(Alternative Route. For a more adventurous route keep ahead at Wp.6 following the walk description from Wp.12 To Wp.16 in walk No.15. (Note this is only possible two hours either side of low tide).

Passing the welcoming **Sportsman's Rest** pub, we go through the village. At the top of a slope, by a fingerpost, we turn left over a stile on CB12a (Wp.7 33M), along the top of a meadow. Following the right hedge line, we cross stiles either side of two more meadows. After crossing two closely spaced stiles, we rise, turning right just below a farm (Wp.8 43M), on a fenced path, to cross a stile to a road (Wp.9 44M). Turning left, we gently climb, bearing left up a concrete road, and turning right at a fingerpost by a clump of large pine trees on CB24 (Wp.10 46M), an attractive grassy path.

Crossing a stile and plank bridge (Wp.11 48M), we bear right by some holiday homes, before turning left along an access road (Wp.12 49M) into a holiday park. We soon fork left on the one-way system (Wp.13 50M), passing through bollards between a shop and an entertainment centre, to descend with **Thorness Bay** ahead. Leaving the park, we turn left at a half barrier gate (Wp.14 54M), on a grass path to the shoreline near the edge of a wood (Wp.15 57M).

Thorness Bay

We turn right behind the beach, soon dropping to walk along the foreshore of the attractive and peaceful bay. Crossing a concrete bridge, we turn left by a fingerpost (Wp.16 69M), to continue along the rear of the beach. A double stile appears at the top of the right bank (Wp.17 71M). We climb, crossing the double stile, turning left along the low cliff top. We follow the **Coastal Path**, crossing stiles, bridges, and negotiating the inevitable landslips of the eroding coastline.

Eventually we descend to **Gurnard Bay**, crossing a stile (Wp.18 102M) and turning right along a track to a road, then left over a sluice gate bridge and creek (Wp.19 103M). We immediately turn left by a fingerpost on CS35, then right along the sea wall and foreshore (this path may be closed but it is possible to walk along the foreshore, tide permitting - the alternative route is to stay on the road from Wp.19). At the end of the main sea wall, by a steel post (Wp.20 107M), we turn right, inland, re-joining the road and turning left (Wp.21 108M). Climbing to a T-junction (Wp.22 113M), we turn left, down **Worsley Road**, and after a series of white bollards, by a fingerpost, turn left down **Winding Way** (Wp.23 115M). At a T-junction, we turn left again, down **Shore Road**, turning right at the bottom onto the promenade (Wp.24 117M).

starting cannons

We follow a series of very fine promenades, with wonderful **Solent** views, and always a chance of viewing merchant shipping and cruise ships. We pass **Egypt Point**, and the Royal Yacht Squadron HQ, built on the foundations of a Tudor castle.

It is possible that the 24 brass starting cannons from the yacht of William IVth will be on display (be aware that the cannons may be fired without warning during racing. During Cowes week, the esplanades are thronged with spectators and competitors - a wonderful people watch, combined with some spectacular sailing from the world's best.

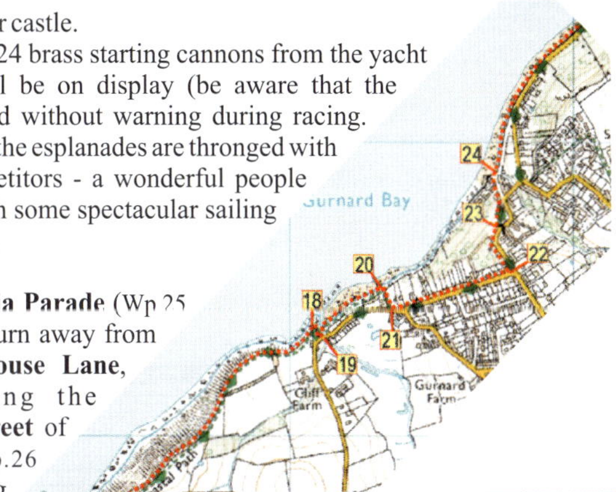

At the end of **Victoria Parade** (Wp.25 143M), we have to turn away from the sea, up **Watchouse Lane**, turning left along the fascinating **High Street** of **West Cowes** (Wp.26 144M). We pass along a pedestrianised

Cowes Week

section, then a road section (buses to **Newport** may be caught from the Red Funnel Terminal on the left). Another pedestrianised section takes us to a junction with **Beckford Road**, where we keep left along **Birmingham Road**, before turning left down **Medina Road**, opposite the **Duke of York** (Wp.27 152M), to the **Floating Bridge** (Wp.28 155M).

The chain ferry across the **River Medina** is a quirky delight - free for foot passengers, and a fascinating and enjoyable experience. On the opposite side, we alight, turning left along **Castle Street** (Wp.29 163M), passing the **Ship and Castle** pub, a real local with no frills. Taking the next right (Wp.30 164M), passing shops, we go over a road junction to the bus stop outside **East Cowes Town Hall** (Wp.31 167M).

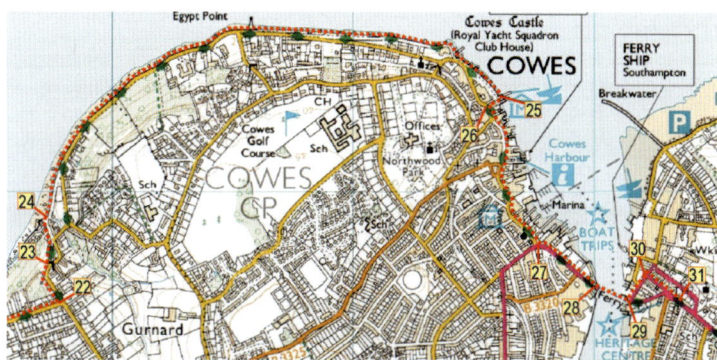

From the very fine **Crown Inn**, **Shorewell**, we go through the haunted **Troopers Wood**, passing the superb **Wolverton Manor** to start a cross-country footpath jaunt to **Chale Green**. We climb the north end of **St Catherine's Down** to visit **Hoy's Monument**, then proceed along a lovely hillside path overlooking the beautiful valley setting across **Downcourt Farm**, before climbing over **Head Down** and descending the ancient track of **Bury Lane** into the charming village of **Niton**, where the **White Lion Inn** should be open all day.

Short Walks:
(a) **Shorewell** to Wp.21 at **Chale Green** (return on bus No.6) (1 hour 25 mins, 4.2 miles/6.8km).
(b) **Chale Green** to **Niton** (bus No.6 to **Chale Green** to the start at Wp.21) (1 hour 15 mins, 3.1 miles/5km).

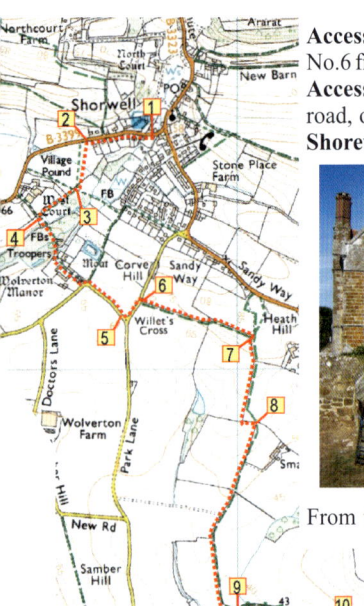

Access by bus: No.7 to **Shorewell**, return on No.6 from **Niton**.
Access by car: Roadside parking on the **Chale** road, off the mini-roundabout by the church in **Shorewell**, bus No.6 and 7 back.

Wolverton Manor

From the **Crown Inn** car park (Wp.1 0M), we head west, up the road, turning left over a stile by the National Speed Limit signs (Wp.2 3M), and crossing a meadow to go over a valley bottom stile (Wp.3 6M) with a worrying array of yellow arrows. Turning right, following the right fence line, we cross a stile and plank bridge, and before a field gate in a corner (Wp.4

9M), we turn left, to follow the right fence down. Crossing a stile and plank bridge over a stream, we enter **Troopers Wood** - thankfully with a wooden walkway (for this wood is said to be haunted with the steps of a Civil War trooper who sank to his death in the wetland bog!).

Emerging behind **Wolverton Manor**, we turn right, bearing left over the nearby plank bridge to pass through a gate and up a tarmac access road through the magnificent farm buildings of the Manor. At a road junction we keep ahead, uphill, turning left at the next junction (Wp.5 18M). In 80m we turn right, near a fingerpost, on SW20 (Wp.6 19M) - a rising grassy path with fine views opening out. After climbing a steep slope, we emerge into a field and follow the left rising hedge line. Cresting the brow of a hill, we drop to a gap between hedges, turning sharply right (Wp.7 26M), to follow the right curving hedge line. At the field corner, maintaining direction, we descend, crossing a track to follow the left fence line, and turning left at the next field corner. In 50m, we turn right, through a gate (Wp.8 30M), onto a path between fences, passing through a bridleway gate, then a field gate, along a low ridge with pleasing subdued views.

At a T-junction with a road, we pass through a gate turning left (Wp.9 39M), and as we approach **Dungewood Farm**, we turn right by a fingerpost, crossing a double stile on SW36 (Wp.10 42M). The right hedge line takes us to a field corner (Wp.11 44M), where we turn left, still tracking the right hedge towards a tree clad **Warren Hill**. Crossing two stiles at a shallow corner (Wp.12 47M), we go over an arable field, in the indicated direction. We cross a stile in the fence line at the shallow valley bottom, before rising to go over a stile, visible at the foot of the hill.

We climb for 20m before bearing right on a faint path, to wind around the lower flanks of the gorse-covered hill, loosely paralleling the right fence. We aim for a marker post at a T-junction with a track (Wp.13 54M), where we turn right to descend to another marker post (Wp.14 55M). Here, we turn left, across an arable field, aiming for the left end of a hedge line.

Keeping ahead to cross a small, lush, meadow, we go over a double stile bridge (Wp.15 57M), before turning left alongside a reed fringed brook. We cross another stile, and pass a recently dug pond embankment, before crossing a plank bridge, maintaining direction to pass a marker post and go diagonally over a large arable field. At the far side we bear left (Wp.16 66M), following the fence past a fingerpost. We keep ahead to join a track, which becomes a rising tarmac access road, and soon turn left by a fingerpost on C24 (Wp.17 73M). Crossing a stile, we go over an arable field to a road (Wp.18 76M), where we turn left, and in 25m, right, crossing a stile onto C33 along the left edge of a meadow. As the fence line deviates left, we bear slightly right, towards a house, crossing a stile (Wp.19 80M) and dropping to a

Hoy's Monument

track to turn left downhill. We emerge at a road (Wp.20 82M), and turn left to **Chale Green** Post Office Stores (Wp.21 83M), the finish and start of the short walks.

Passing the shop, we keep ahead over the junction with **Town Lane**, to cross a white-railed stream bridge, then turn right by a fingerpost up C1 (Wp.22 84M), paralleling the deep cut stream to our right. We keep ahead, crossing three stiles, proceeding over a bridleway crossroads (Wp.23 94M), and up a delightful rising wooded path to pass through a steel gate. Keeping to the obvious path, we climb to go through a small gate (Wp.24 103M), bearing right to the nearby fingerpost, then forking left on C6 (Wp.25 104M), sharply uphill. We turn left through a gate (Wp.26 106M), onto a grass path, to visit **Hoy's Monument**, erected in 1814 to commemorate the visit of Tsar Alexander 1st, and with an additional tablet added in 1857 in memory of British soldiers killed in the Crimean War.

We resume on the grass path to a nearby fingerpost (Wp.27 109M), by a fence corner, turning left, steeply downhill through a wood. Before a pair of wooden gates (Wp.28 111M), we turn right, loosely following the left fence line - a superb path through the downland landscape. At a junction with a grassy track (Wp.29 120M), we turn hard left, through a gate, descending to a cluster of three gates (Wp.30 122M), where we turn left, passing above **Downcourt Farm**.

We drop to go through a gate (Wp.31 124M), turning right, now passing the farm on a track, and maintaining direction over a shallow dip. 60m after a second shallow dip in the track, at a hedge corner (Wp.32 130M), we bear half left over an arable field to climb up to and cross a stile (Wp.33 133M). We initially follow the right fence up, before turning half left, traversing up the steep hillside towards the trees on the summit. Crossing a stile (Wp.34 138M), we turn right to go over another, then turn left for 15m before turning right again on a slightly rising grass path between bushes, **Bury Lane** (Wp.35 140M).

The descending track becomes a tree tunnel towards the bottom, leading on to a tarmac lane, and down to a T-junction with a road (Wp.36 151M). Turning left, into **Niton**, we pass the **Ventnor** bound bus stop (the **Newport** bound bus stop is just down **Rectory Lane** opposite), and turn right at the crossroads (Wp.37 153M) to the **White Lion Inn** (Wp.38 154M).

19. Chale Bay

From the lovely setting of **Chale Church** (c1114), we pass through the village, once the smuggling capital of the Island, to cross the lower slopes of **St Catherine's Down**. Climbing to a delightful elevated path along **South Down**, we descend to cross a farming landscape to **Shepherds Chine**. The stunning and magnificent cliff top path, takes us to **Whale**

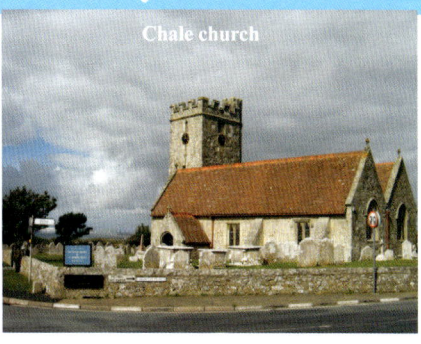
Chale church

Chine before returning to **Chale** and the **Wight Mouse Inn**.

3 | 3 H | 8.1 miles/13km | 210m / 210m | ⚠ | ↻ 3 | 🍴 3

Access by bus: No.6 to **Chale Church** (**Wight Mouse Inn**).
Access by car: Limited roadside parking, or the **Wight Mouse Inn** car park with permission.

From the bus stop (Wp.1 0M), we pass the **Wight Mouse Inn**, turning right on a bend opposite a green scout hut, into **Upper House Lane** (Wp.2 3M). At the top, we bear left, up a track C9 (Wp.3 6M), passing through a bridleway gate (Wp.4 8M) and bearing right on a rising path between hedges. Opening out into a meadow, we follow the obvious path, diagonally, to a raised hedge just below a marker post (Wp.5 15M), and turn hard left, downhill. Loosely following the right fence/hedge line, with glorious views across the south west coast, we cross a stile, then another in the

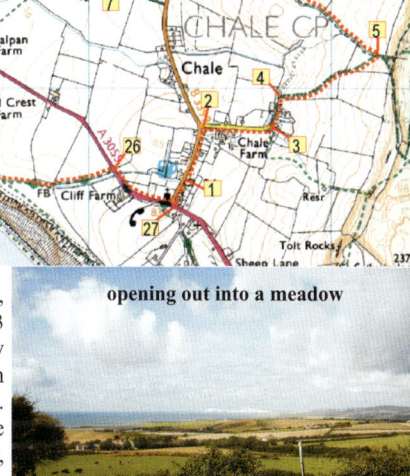
opening out into a meadow

bottom right corner. Now loosely following the left hedge line down, we go over stiles either end of a narrow descending meadow onto a track, emerging to cross a road and a stile opposite onto footpath C21 (Wp.6 37M).

Passing a pump house, now following the right hedge/ditch line, we cross a farm track (Wp.7 41M), still tracking the ditch to go over a sleeper bridge and stile in a corner. We keep ahead over two more stiles, passing to the right of a cottage, joining a track and turning hard right at a road (Wp.8 48M), to climb a steep footpath C22, between hedges. This gem of a path, along **South Down**, crosses a small clearing to descend, through a gate (Wp.9 56M), to a road, where we keep right. Crossing a road junction (Wp.10 59M), we keep ahead on C28, alongside a fence to go through a small gate into woodland. Passing through the back garden of **Pyle Manor**, we maintain direction on a lovely woodland path, going through a field gate and bearing right, uphill, for 25m before forking left by a fingerpost. Deer are not native to the Island, but you may see a captive herd behind the high fence on the hill to the right.

Continuing along the top edge of the beautiful woodland, we descend to cross a footbridge and fine wooden walkway through an unexpected wetland wood. Emerging over a stile, we cross a clearing to the top right corner, going over two more stiles to a fingerpost T-junction with a track by a small green barn (Wp.11 72M). We turn left on C26, initially descending, and keeping ahead at a fingerpost on C25. After a slight rise, we fork half right (Wp.12 79M), diagonally crossing a large arable field, passing through a makeshift gate to go by a marker post, and on over a plank footbridge. A path between hedges takes us over a stile, following a reed-lined ditch. At a stile, we turn right, crossing the double stile bridge (Wp.13 86M) and turning left along a lush field edge. As the long narrow field opens out, we bear half right, diagonally crossing to follow the right hedge line to a T-junction with a concrete farm road (Wp.14 90M). Turning left, up towards **Little Atherfield Farm**, we then turn right, around the perimeter of the farm, to emerge at a road, where we turn right again (Wp.15 94M).

Just past **Home Farm**, as the road bears right, we turn left by a fingerpost (Wp.16 97M), soon forking right up farm track SW24. Passing a stone cottage, we maintain direction through a bridleway gate, crossing between open fields on a track, which bears right toward a white thatched cottage (Wp.17 104M).

the clifftop path

Bearing left before the cottage, we reach the **Military Road** by a fingerpost, turning right along the verge (Wp.18 107M). Passing over the top end of **Shepherds Chine**, we turn left, crossing the road, to go through a fence by a fingerpost on SW25 (Wp.19 108M).

We pass down the right field edge, before descending the chine to turn left at a **Coastal Path** fingerpost (Wp.20 111M). Climbing steps, we turn right at the top, to find the fabulous cliff top path, along a continually eroding coastline, with terrific views. At **Whale Chine**, passing the amazingly steep steps to the beach, (allegedly inaccessible due to land movement, but perhaps a challenge for the adventurous walker?), we head inland (Wp.21 151M). At the car park we turn right (Wp.22 155M), along the verge of the **Military Road**, and right again, by a fingerpost (Wp.23 159M), crossing an arable field to regain the cliff top path (Wp.24 163M).

Whale Chine steps

We reach the smaller, but still impressive, **Walpen Chine**, curving landwards alongside the **Chine** as it transforms to a ditch. Our path crosses the ditch (Wp.25 173M), which we follow to a footbridge. Crossing, and turning right, we continue to follow the ditch up to the **Military Road** (Wp.26 180M). Here, we may cross, taking the car park road to the **Wight Mouse Inn**, or alternatively, turn right, along the verge, to pass through **Chale** churchyard (Wp.28 183M), turning left to return to the bus stops (Wp.1 184M).

20. Shorewell and the Downs

From the **Crown Inn** through the attractive village of **Shorewell**, for a mainly downland walk, with enough superb views to more than satisfy the discerning hill walker.

3 | 3H | 8.4 miles/13.5km | 320m 320m | 4

Short Walks:

(a) Turn right at Wp.6 through a bridleway gate, descending to join up with the **Worsley Trail** and re-join the route passing through the bridleway gate at Wp.24 by the disused pit. (1 hour 10 mins, 3.1 miles/5 km)

(b) Turn right at Wp.8, soon descending to re-join the route keeping ahead on the terraced track at Wp.16. (2 hours 20 mins, 6.3 miles/10.1 km)

Access by bus: No.7 alighting at the **Crown Inn** bus stop.

Access by car: Roadside parking on the **Chale** road, off the mini-roundabout by the church in **Shorewell**.

Crown Inn

From the **Crown Inn** bus stop (Wp.1 0M), we negotiate the mini-roundabout, passing the church, and taking the left footway. Passing through the village, with its Post Office and attractive cottages, we turn half right at a road junction (Wp.2 5M) up bridleway S13, alongside a terrace of thatched cottages. After a bridleway gate, we bear right along a meadow (Wp.3 6M), to pass through another gate around the lower slopes of **Mount Ararat**. As a grassy farm track drops away to our right, we keep left on a path along the top of a short bank to pass through two bridleway gates, then another (Wp.4 16M), turning right to follow a farm track. After a track joins from our right, we cross a cattle grid, climbing the stone-surfaced track, as fine views progressively unfurl.

Turning right at a T-junction (Wp.5 23M), we follow a concrete access road along **Northcourt Down**, with pleasing all-round views. As we approach the transmitter aerial, we leave the road, forking left on bridleway N146 (Wp.6 33M) (for short walk (a) turn right through the bridleway gate). The gently rising farm track, along the downland tops, takes us past a dew-pond (quite a rarity on the Island) and a pair of corrugated barns (Wp.7 44M), as we proceed through a field gate to follow the right fence line on a charming grass track. We pass through another gate onto a stunning track, along the top of **Dukem Copse**. Keeping ahead at a bridleway fingerpost junction (Wp.8 53M) (for short walk (b) turn right), and through a sparse pine wood, we emerge to fabulous panoramic views.

After a bridleway gate (Wp.9 59M), we loosely follow the right fence line down, going through another gate before descending along the edge of **Barcham's Copse**. A bridleway gate drops us through a copse to a T-junction

(Wp.10 69M), we keep left, with the overgrown remains of a limekiln to our left, following the track down to a T-junction at the shallow valley bottom and turning right (Wp.11 70M). With **Carisbrooke Castle** on the skyline and fine all-round views, we keep ahead, turning right at the next T-junction (Wp.12 73M) on a gently climbing farm track, going through a bridleway gate.

gently climbing farm track

After passing a stone barn, we turn right at a T-junction of tracks (Wp.13 84M), going through a nearby bridleway gate, continuing ahead up the left track between a disused pit and a sunken track, before curving steeply left to a marker post (Wp.14 88M). We turn left, climbing to go through a gate onto bridleway G7, the incidence of fine views rapidly increasing on this scenic terraced

owing the right fence line

merging from the sparse pine wood

the Ramson path

track. Passing through a bridleway gate by a fingerpost (Wp.15 99M), we descend sharply on a grass path to turn left at a nearby fingerpost T-junction with a terraced track (Wp.16 100M). The track becomes a sunken path before reverting to a farm track, curving round to pass **New Barn Farm**. As the farm road turns sharply left, we continue ahead on a farm track, signed bridleway G6 (Wp.17 109M), gently climbing a field edge to a T-junction of tracks (Wp.18 116M) where we turn right, up a rising woodland track. After passing a gate, we soon fork left by a fingerpost onto footpath G7 (Wp.19 117M), through a dense carpet of ramsons (the woodland around **Shorewell** is pungent with the aroma of ramsons in May).

Emerging from the wood, we cross a stile, turning left, then right over an access land stile (Wp.20 121M), doubling back. We climb the slope for 50m then turn left, loosely contouring, before gently climbing to a stile in the fence-line ahead beside a clump of seven windblown, stunted trees. Crossing

wind-blown tree on ridge

the access land stile (Wp.21 130M), we head towards the TV mast, passing the **Five Barrows** earthwork (Wp.22 134M) of **Chillerton Down** on our right, an Iron Age rampart, sadly concealed by hawthorn scrub.

We continue across the organic downland, making for a stile in the fence-line to the left of the mast (Wp.23 142M).

Crossing, we maintain direction, picking up a sheep track along the slope, and passing above a series of three large posts before dropping down to the far left field corner by a very attractive grass clothed pit. Passing through a bridleway gate (Wp.24 149M), we briefly join the **Worsley Trail** on a track between hedges before turning hard right at a T-junction onto bridleway G13 (Wp.25 151M), following the right hedge line uphill between arable fields. At a field corner, ignoring a path that drops to our left, we bear right, initially between hedges, then impressively along the ridge, with views that delight all around.

Passing through two bridleway gates (Wp.26 165M), we keep ahead to cross a stile. Ignoring several garden gates, we descend to cross over a stile, passing through ramson-rich woodland, and over another stile (Wp.27 177M) to emerge back at the road in **Shorewell** (Wp.28 178M). Turning left, we retrace our steps to the **Crown Inn** (Wp.1 184M), perhaps via the fine church with its 15th century wall painting and many other notable features.

21. Carisbrooke Castle and Gatcombe

Carisbrooke was the Saxon and Medieval capital until the 16th century, when **Newport** took over. The Norman Castle, notable for its still working donkey well, sunk in 1130, stands on a late Roman fort. Charles 1st was held captive here for 4 years until taken to **London** to have his head removed.

We start from the imposing **Carisbrooke Church**, passing down **Castle Street** to a ford, before climbing up for a first visit to the Castle. A charming path takes us along **Lukely Brook** water meadows before climbing the magnificent **Dukem Down**, for wonderful views. We pass through the peaceful hamlet of **Gatcombe** with its church and cottages, climb up to the panoramic hills, passing a geological quirk, and down the atmospheric **Dark Lane**. On our second visit to the Castle, we have the opportunity to appreciate the huge scale of the fortifications, before returning to the **High Street**.

3 | 2½H | 7 miles/11.3km | 330m / 330m | 3

ShortWalk: Carisbrooke, **Dukem Down** and **Gatcombe** Tearooms. Follow the route to Wp.17, turning left down the tarmac lane at **Newbarn Farm**, passing the Tea Gardens to rejoin the walk at Wp.21 (2 hours 10 mins, 5.5 miles/8.9km)

Access by bus: No.38 or 7 to **Carisbrooke** High Street, by the church.
Access by car: Park in the Castle car park, commencing the walk at Wp.4.

Carisbrooke church

From the **Newport** bound bus stop in **Carisbrooke** High Street (Wp.1 0M), we climb the steps to visit the imposing 12th century church, with its magnificent 1470 tower, flagstone floor, and a fascinating 13th century stone coffin in the porch. Exiting the church, we go down steps, dropping to the road, and crossing to go down **Castle Street** opposite (Wp.2 1M). At the bottom, we pass alongside a remarkably lengthy ford, before bearing right into **Millers Lane**, passing **Castle Lane**, and turning left by a fingerpost on N191 (Wp.3 6M). Crossing a rustic stile, the steep path takes us over another stile and up steps to turn right, past the castle entrance.

At the car park entrance gates (Wp.4 10M), we bear right, to a fingerpost, down N88 to a road (Wp.5 13M), where we turn right, and immediately fork left. We descend, turning left over a stile and footbridge on N104 (Wp.6 14M), to a charming footpath alongside Lukely Brook water meadows and marsh. Crossing a stile near a redundant sheep dip, then three further stiles, we turn left up a hedge-lined bridleway (Wp.7 30M), and in 55m turn right up steps and over a stile (Wp.8 31M) on a path

castle entrance

between arable fields. Turning left at a track T-junction (Wp.9 38M), we turn right at the next T-junction (Wp.10 39M), and then turn left at a marker post by **Frogland Copse** (Wp.11 44M).

Our path rises to pass a disused lime kiln, and we bear right in the corner, up N146 (Wp.12 45M), through a short copse, from which we emerge through a gate. A steady climb following the left fence of **Barcham's Copse**, rewards us with fantastic views opening out across a deep valley. Ascending to pass through two bridleway gates (Wp.13 61M), new views appear to the south, as we pass a clump of pine trees on a lovely track along the top of **Dukem Down**.

At a fingerpost, we turn left on G22 (Wp.14 65M), leaving the trees through a gate, to follow the left

fine view of the eastern Downs

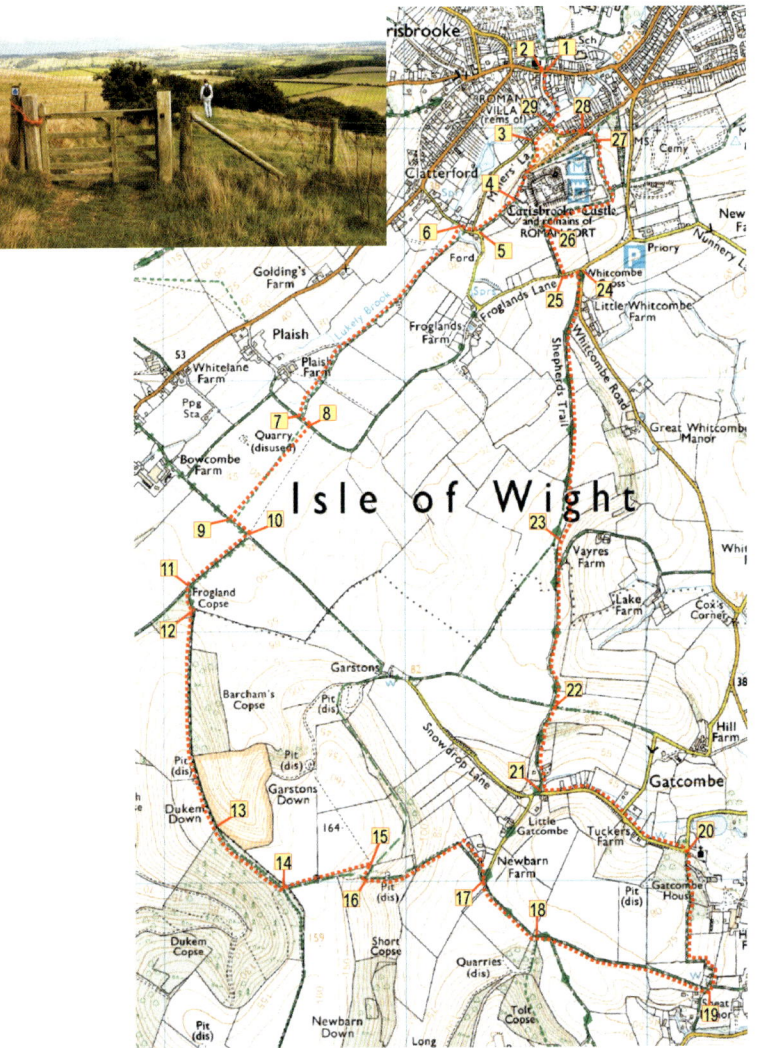

fence, with another series of superb views appearing towards **Sandown Bay** and the eastern Downs. Passing a dew pond, relatively uncommon on the Island, we descend through a bridleway gate, on a delightful path, following the fence to a fingerpost by a gate (Wp.15 72M), and then turning hard right, downhill, to a nearby fingerpost at a T-junction with a track (Wp.16 73M). Turning left down G7, a fine terraced track, we pass through a cutting before bearing right, past **Newbarn Farm**. Then, as the access road bears sharply left (Wp.17 80M), we keep ahead on the main farm track G6.

We pass up the left field edge, keeping left at a T-junction (Wp.18 85M), and passing a nearby fingerpost, still on the main farm track. Descending to a T-junction, we turn left on G11 (Wp.19 94M), and keep left rising to pass two stone cottages. A hedge-lined path zig-zags, before descending through a lovely wood emerging at a road (Wp.20 102M), giving us the option to visit the 13thC **Gatcombe** Church, with notable William Morris windows above the altar.

a rocky outcrop

Dark Lane

We turn left, passing **Tuckers Farm** and several charming thatched cottages. As the lane swings left, by a corrugated barn, to **Gatcombe** Tearooms, we turn right, up an access drive by a fingerpost on G6 (Wp.21 109M), passing a cottage and keeping ahead up a steep slope. At a fingerpost (Wp.22 115M), we keep ahead, following a left hedge line to go through a bridleway gate next to a field gate. Wonderful views open out as we loosely follow the left hedge, curiously perched along the top of a rocky outcrop, before going through another bridleway gate. Our path keeps ahead taking us by two fingerposts (Wp.23 124M), before descending into a shady cutting, **Dark Lane** - an atmospheric sunken path of ancient origin, which heads directly towards **Carisbrooke**.

Emerging, the Castle comes into view, and we turn left at a road junction (Wp.24 136M), turning right in 90m by a hidden fingerpost (Wp.25 137M). The footpath sinks between very high hedges, so we keep to the field for better views, joining the path at the top left corner (Wp.26 141M) and climbing sharply up the outer castle bank. Turning right at the top, the impressive scale of the fortifications becomes apparent, as we pass along two sides of the outer ditch. At the second corner (Wp.27 150M), with the keep visible away to our left, we drop through the trees and down two flights of stone steps to a road. Turning left, we cross, passing down **Castle Lane** (Wp.28 151M) and turning right at the bottom (Wp.29 153M), re-tracing our outward route, past the ford and up to the **High Street**, turning right for the bus stops (Wp.1 157M). Up the hill to the left is the recommended **Waverly** pub, and to the right the **Eight Bells**.

22. Hoy's Monument and St Catherine's Down

From the charming village of **Niton**, we climb over **Head Down**, taking in some delightful paths through this exceptionally beautiful area. We climb to visit **Hoy's Monument**, before walking along the ridge of **St Catherine's Down**, with wonderful views as we ascend to the second highest point on the Island and the Medieval '**Pepperpot**' lighthouse. Returning along the top of **Gore Cliff**, the **Coastal Path** passes above **St Catherine's Lighthouse**, before we head inland back to **Niton** and the **White Lion Inn**.

Access by bus: No.6 to **Niton**, (**Church Street** from **Newport**, **Rectory Road** from **Ventnor**).

Access by car: Roadside parking on the one-way **Blackgang Road**.

From the crossroads in the village centre (Wp.1 0M), we go up **Church Street**, turning right before the church, up Pan Lane (Wp.2 1M), and then right again by a fingerpost on NT54 (Wp.3 4M). Passing through **Ladyacre Farm** on a rising track, we cross a stile by a field gate. Turning left to follow the right fence line uphill, we pass through a field gate with stile, bearing right along the lower edge of a meadow. By a marker post and stile in the right hedge (Wp.4 12M), we bear left up the meadow, to make for and cross a stile (Wp.5 13M), which appears in the right hedge as we climb. A grass path between hedges takes us to a T-junction to turn left (Wp.6 15M), and in 30m by a marker post, we turn right, crossing a stile, initially following the right hedge, then cutting the corner to cross a stile ahead into gorse bushes.

a 'gorse bush' stile

With beautiful views over the valley ahead, we descend **Head Down** through the gorse, following the obvious path, crossing a stile (Wp.7 22M). Maintaining direction, we diagonally cross a narrow meadow, meandering down to cross another stile onto a shady track. At the bottom (Wp.8 26M), the track bears right, high above a stream - a gem of a path, centuries old. By a field gate, we turn left over a concrete bridge (Wp.9 33M), on a tree lined path up the opposite valley side, crossing a farm track, and then keeping ahead to climb up to, and go through, a field gate into a meadow. Passing up the left side of an overgrown track to the top of a slope, we drop into a sunken track to go through a field gate, and in 15m turn left up another fine, tree lined, track (Wp.10 41M).

a gem of a path

We go through a bridleway gate, up the left side of a meadow, and then through another gate, passing a white cottage, before turning right by a fingerpost on GL26 (Wp.11 52M). This delightful woodland path soon follows a substantial stone wall to a corner, where we turn left, along a wood edge, with fine views to **Stenbury Down** and **Gat Cliff**.

Turning right, down an access road (Wp.12 56M), we then turn hard left, back on ourselves, through a bridleway gate by a fingerpost (Wp.13 59M). We climb a pasture and pass to the left of two electricity pylons to go through two closely spaced bridleway gates. Bearing left at a junction of paths (Wp.14 64M), we rise to fork left at a fingerpost (Wp.15 65M), up a sunken track, and then turn left again through a bridleway gate (Wp.16 68M) to visit **Hoy's Monument** (Wp.17 69M). (Erected 1814 to commemorate the visit of Tsar Alexander 1st, with an additional tablet added in 1857 in memory of British soldiers killed in the Crimean War.).

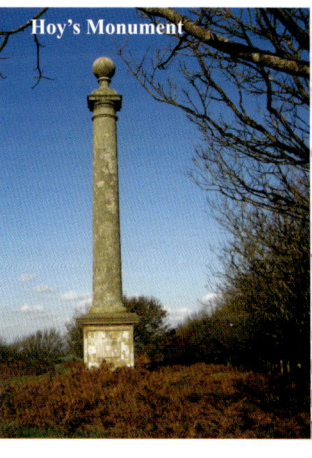
Hoy's Monument

We turn right at the Monument, on a delightful grass path along the ridge, with stunning views both sides, heading towards the distant '**Pepperpot**'. Passing through a gate by a fingerpost (Wp.18 83M), we bear left, on the well-worn path up to **St Catherine's Oratory** and Medieval lighthouse (Wp.19 90M), reminiscent of 'Flash Gordon's' space ship!

the 'Pepperpot'

After a ship ran aground on **Atherfield Ledge** in 1314, the sailors escaped the wreck, and making the most of their misfortune, sold the cargo of 174 casks of wine to various islanders. Walter de Godeton was prosecuted and found guilty for receiving 53 casks of stolen wine, as the cargo was not the sailors' to sell. However, the wine actually belonged to a religious community in Picardy who lodged a complaint in the Rome court, and de Godeton was ordered to build a lighthouse to warn ships, along with an oratory for a priest, who would trim the lighthouse lamps and say masses for the souls lost at sea. The oratory foundations are now barely visible but the 'Pepperpot' lighthouse remains, close to several round barrows of the Bronze Age.

Passing the '**Pepperpot**', with wonderful views along the south west coast from the second highest point on the Island, we turn half right, to climb a stile

above Gore Cliff

in the fence below (Wp.20 91M). Heading down a grass path to cross another stile, we maintain direction across a meadow, to go through a kissing gate by a fingerpost. Dropping down steps, we cross the road (Wp.21 97M), passing through the car park and climbing a flight of concrete steps at the end to join the **Coastal Path**. At the cliff top we turn left (Wp.22 99M), passing above **Blackgang Chine** and along the top of the spectacular **Gore Cliff**, eventually with **St Catherine's Lighthouse** below.

Passing a fingerpost at the top of steps (Wp.23 114M), we continue, going through kissing gates either side of a meadow, and immediately turning left through a third gate (Wp.24 122M), to follow the right fence line. Crossing a stile, we bear slightly left to drop down a cleft at the field edge, and climb a stile onto a fine descending path through trees down to the road (Wp.25 128M). Turning right, we return to the village of **Niton**, passing the **White Lion Inn** (Wp.26 132M), and turning left to find the bus stops at the crossroads (Wp.1 133M).

From the charming village centre of **Niton**, we cross the Downs to pass along **Gore Cliff** – evidence of landslip of the undercliff laid out, spectacularly, before us. Making our way through the National Trust landslip, we pass **St Catherines Lighthouse** and along the coast before heading inland, climbing past the **Buddle Inn**. A very unusual footpath takes us back towards **Niton** and the **White Lion Inn**.

Access by bus: No.6 from **Newport**, or from **Ventnor** to the village centre crossroads.
Access by car: Roadside parking on the one-way **Blackgang Road**.

Leaving the village crossroads bus stops (Wp.1 0M), we head for the nearby **White Lion**, turning right past the Inn (Wp.2 1M). We make our way up the one-way system towards **Blackgang**. As the road bends left, leaving the village, we bear right by a fingerpost on bridleway NT52 (Wp.3 5M) - a pleasing path, which climbs round the lower slopes of **Niton Down**.

At a T-junction with a tarmac track (Wp.4 17M), we turn left, and in 30m turn half right over a stile, crossing a field to pass through a nearby gate at a road (Wp.5 19M). Turning right, along the verge, we cross to a fingerpost onto footpath C11, passing over a field to a stile on the skyline (Wp.6 23M). A panorama of the southwest coast appears as we cross the stile and turn left along the unprotected cliff top **Coastal Path**, with the delights of **Blackgang Chine** below. The path takes us along the magnificent **Gore Cliff**, haunt of jackdaws, ravens, and buzzards, to eventually arrive at a fingerpost (Wp.7 37M).

the stile at the Coastal Path

High above **St Catherine's Lighthouse**, we turn hard right, down a long flight of steps on a beautiful path, weaving down through the landslip woodland, and emerging to turn right along the **Old Blackgang Road** (Wp.8 42M). At a car park, beyond which the road disappeared in a massive landslip of 1928, we go through a kissing gate on the left (Wp.9 46M). Keeping left on the grass path, we soon drop to a large stone outcrop (Wp.10 47M), and turn left along a shallow valley, surprisingly reminiscent of the Peak District.

Gore Cliff

At a fork of paths (Wp.11 49M) we bear right, up a slope, turning left along the secondary cliff edge (Wp.12 50M) with the lighthouse below. Keeping to the right of a prominent rock outcrop (Wp.13 54M), we meander down, turning right at the bottom corner, crossing a stile, and turning right again down an access road (Wp.14 58M). As the road bears left towards the lighthouse (Wp.15 60M), we keep ahead, on the track, towards **Knowles Farm** - once the home of Marconi. Note the dry stone walls, unusual on the island, which utilise the abundance of naturally occurring sandstone.

large stone outcrop

Passing the farm, we cross a stile by a field gate (Wp.16 62M), turning left to follow the fence line down, and left again, over a stile above the sea shore (Wp.17 63M). The path skirts round the landward side of the lighthouse,

stile above the seashore

crossing two staircase stiles (Wp.18 65M), before returning to the coast and along the low cliff top (Wp.19 67M). Passing through a kissing gate, and a clutch of caravans, we bear left up a stony access road (Wp.20 74M). Soon after a hairpin bend (Wp.21 76M), by a bench seat, we turn left up a challenging flight of steps (Wp.22 77M), then right on reaching a road, with the welcome option to visit the **Buddle Inn** (Wp.23 82M).

Continuing up the road to a T-junction, we cross onto a footpath by a stone wall (Wp.24 89M). Steadily climbing the amazingly distinctive shady path, almost claustrophobically hemmed in by high stone walls, and passing through two stone tunnels, we emerge, to turn right, up a driveway. In 25m we turn hard right on NT29 footpath (Wp.25 94M), along the high secondary cliff top, with views of sea and Downs opening out.

the Buddle Inn

By a fingerpost (Wp.26 104M), we turn hard left on NT27, with a fine view of **Niton**, as we diagonally cross a field, over a stile, dropping by a fingerpost (Wp.27 108M) to cross another field and along a hedge-lined path. Reaching a four way fingerpost, at a 5-way junction of paths (Wp.28 112M), we keep ahead, bearing right, and then keeping ahead again at a T-junction by a stone cottage (Wp.29 114M). Our path unexpectedly emerges in the village centre, opposite the **White Lion** (Wp.1 115M), and we turn right to return to the bus stops at the village crossroads.

the fingerpost between fields

24. Rookley and the Chequers Inn

A peaceful and charming walk around a less frequented part of the Island, passing through wood, field, hills and farm. From the top of the village, after a fine woodland, we cross the upper reaches of the infant **River Medina**, undulating across farmland to cross back, visiting the **Chequers Inn** and returning over attractive fields.

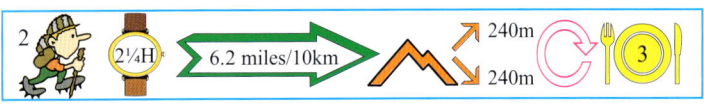

Access by bus: No.2 to **Rookley Old School**.
Access by car: Roadside parking in **Niton Road**, **Rookley**.

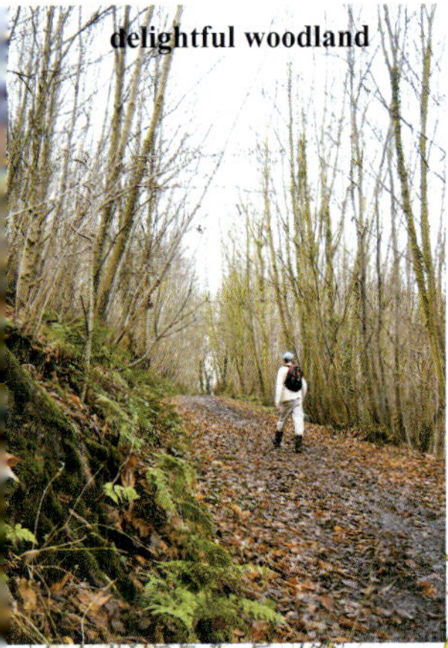

delightful woodland

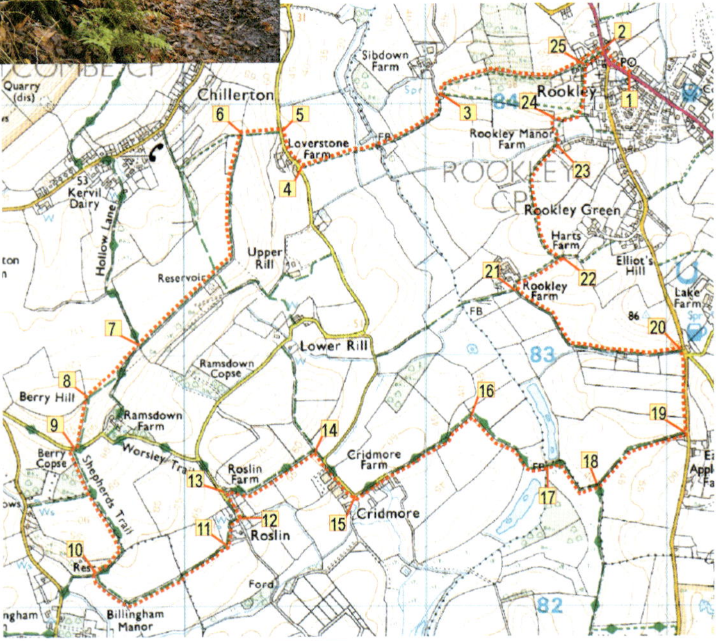

From the bus stop (Wp.1 0M), we head towards **Newport**, and follow the road round a bend, to turn left by a traffic island up **Bunkers Lane** (Wp.2 1M), initially a stony track. Our route takes us through delightful woodland - the damage wrought by the 1987 hurricane still evident from the rotting tree corpses - and turn left over a stile by a fingerpost between gates onto GL1 (Wp.3 10M). Following the right fence line curving down a field, we cross a double stile in the bottom right corner. We keep ahead over a meadow to cross stiles either side of a footbridge, as we go over the stream, which is the young **River Medina**. Bearing half right, we cross a stile in the fence line under a lone oak tree, and go over a large arable field, passing a fingerpost below **Loverstone Farm**, and keeping ahead to turn right at a road (Wp.4 20M).

After a vintage wooden clad granary, and over the top of a rise, we fork left by a fingerpost on G15 (Wp.5 23M), heading uphill, and passing through a scattering of trees to turn left on a rising path following a left hedge line (Wp.6 26M). We go through a bridleway gate, with superb views opening out as we climb the ridge towards **Berry Hill**. Near the summit, we pass to the right side of a fingerpost (Wp.7

post between gates

40M), following the left hedge line, gently climbing with fine downland views. At a patch of scrub we bear left (Wp.8 44M), descending on a track along the lower edge of light woodland, to a road, where we turn right, and in 20m, left, by a fingerpost on G15 (Wp.9 47M), briefly joining the **Shepherds Trail**.

We go down the right side of a field on a descending path, and turn right in a field corner, then immediately left, down a grassy track (Wp.10 56M). At the

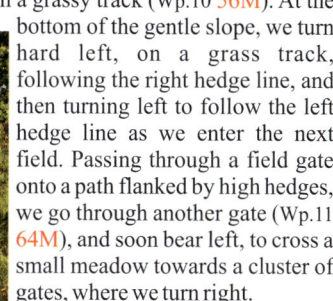
crossing the ford

bottom of the gentle slope, we turn hard left, on a grass track, following the right hedge line, and then turning left to follow the left hedge line as we enter the next field. Passing through a field gate onto a path flanked by high hedges, we go through another gate (Wp.11 64M), and soon bear left, to cross a small meadow towards a cluster of gates, where we turn right.

At an access road (Wp.12 66M), we turn left on G14, passing an attractive farm. We then turn right, still on G14 (Wp.13 67M) - a gravel track, rising to pass through a field gate onto a track along the bottom edge of a large field. At a fingerpost we turn right (Wp.14 72M), keeping ahead along a nearby road, and passing several barns of **Cridmore Farm**. We follow the access road round to the left by a fingerpost on G24 (Wp.15 75M), passing a farmhouse and outbuildings, and keeping ahead up a rising enclosed grassy track. Emerging, we follow a right fence line, descending to cross a corner stile (Wp.16 83M), where we turn right, again following the right fence. Passing between posts into the next field, the obvious grass track curves over a lovely meadow to a choice of double stile **footbridge (Wp.17 89M) for dry feet, or a gate** through a ford for wet!

After crossing the upper **River Medina**, the path turns right, then left, before keeping ahead through a bridleway gate at a fingerpost (Wp.18 93M). We follow a rising, shady, path to a road where we carefully turn left (Wp.19 98M). Using the left verge where possible, we come to the **Chequers Inn** (Wp.20 101M), before turning left down bridleway GL5a, a descending access track with distant **Chillerton Down** ahead.

stile in a field corner

At **Rookley Farm**, we fork right on a gravel drive (Wp.21 117M), soon turning right again to climb a stile by a fingerpost up GL5. We turn left before a stile in the corner (Wp.22 121M), and along the top of a field edge. Passing across another field edge, with fine views, we bear right by a fingerpost, to pass between fence and hedge. We go through a field gate (Wp.23 130M), keeping left to pass through another, and climbing a grass track, again keeping left, to cross a stile in a small field corner (Wp.24 132M). Turning right, we loosely follow the right fence line around two sides of a field, before crossing a corner stile onto a woodland path. At a T-junction with a track (Wp.25 136M), we turn right, re-tracing our steps to the main road, and turning right again to return to the bus stop (Wp.1 139M).

25. River Medina & Newport.

Newport is situated at the highest navigable point of the **River Medina**, the reason for the Town's existence as the Island's capital. Our walk takes us through the older parts of the town, and along the quayside, to head south along the river bank, turning inland at the vintage paddle steamer, the **Ryde Queen**. The old railway line, with Queen Victoria connections, leads us to a pleasing field and wood landscape before we rejoin to 'steam' back into **Newport**, avoiding the 21st century traffic.

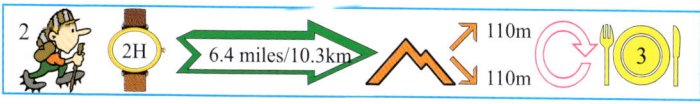

Access by bus: Any bus to **Newport** Bus Station.
Access by car: South Street car park, **Newport**.

From **Newport** Bus Station (Wp.1 0M), we walk back along the terminus entrance road, turning right (Wp.2 1M), crossing the road to go past the **Prince of Wales** pub before turning left along **Town Lane** (Wp.3 2M). Crossing a road, we keep ahead along a short passage and through the charming **St Thomas's Square** to a road junction (Wp.4 4M). We cross, bearing right, past **Watchbell Lane**, into **Quay Street**, soon descending past the 18thC merchants' houses of this fine wide street. At the bottom (Wp.5 7M), we bear left, crossing the road to walk along the quayside, opposite the **Bargemans Rest** pub - the highest navigable part of the **River Medina**.

Keeping to the right of the Jubilee Stores Studio, and passing the entrances to the Bus and Classic Boat Museums, we bear right up footpath N120 (Wp.6 11M). Keeping ahead over an access road to the **Medina Quay** pub, the path takes us through the site of the Newport Music Festival in **Seaclose Park**, close to the riverbank. As the path bears sharp right, we bear left across a small riverside green, onto the riverside path (Wp.7 17M). The attractive path meanders along the bank, crossing bridges, before opening out to lead us past the old paddle steamer, the **Ryde Queen**, withdrawn from the Portsmouth to Ryde service in 1960.

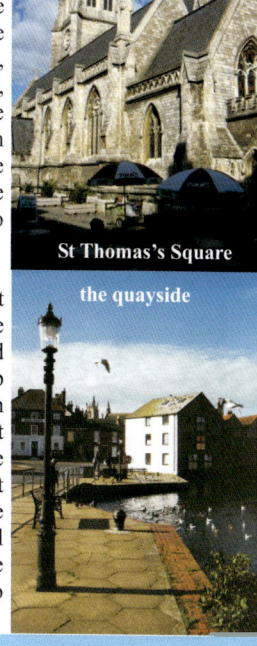

St Thomas's Square

the quayside

Turning right (Wp.8 38M), away from the river, past the **Ryde Queen** bows, away from the river, and the **Harbour Bistro**, we bear right up the access road (Wp.9 43M). Crossing the main road (Wp.10 50M), up a farm track, with glimpses of an amazing collection of letter-boxes in the garden to our left, we turn left before a defunct railway bridge (Wp.11 52M). The path winds up to the old trackbed, where we keep left towards **Wooton**. The tree-lined track leads us to the station of **Whippingham**, the old platform still visible on the right - hard to believe this was the station used by Queen Victoria on her visits to **Osbourne House**.

We turn right (Wp.12 62M), through a kissing gate, into **Fatingpark Copse**, up a rising track. As the main track forks right, we keep ahead through the woodland. At a T-junction (Wp.13 69M), we turn right on a lovely footpath, threading our way along the edge of a long neglected coppice, with May bluebells and June foxgloves abundant. After crossing two stiles, we turn left at a fingerpost T-junction on N116 (Wp.14 74M), passing along the right edge of a large meadow with pleasing low views. We cross a stile onto a tree-lined rising path, emerging to follow a right hedge line across a field. Crossing a stile to a multi-way junction (Wp.15 89M), we turn right, over another stile onto N118, almost immediately forking right on a descending farm track, with **Newport** and the Downs beyond to our left.

Keeping ahead, our track eventually bears right, and we cross a stile by a field gate (Wp.16 93M), dropping down a hedge-lined path. The path bears left by two field gates (Wp.17 96M), becoming a track leading through **Little Fairlee Farm**, and descending towards a road. Just before the road, we turn left (Wp.18 99M), re-joining the old railway line into **Newport**. A shady path soon leads us through the suburbs of the town, as we ignore all crossing paths and roads to drop through a (thankfully) preserved railway tunnel (Wp.19 110M) under the mayhem of traffic above. Emerging, we climb a slope, and drop down the other side to pass a subway (Wp.20 112M) and return to the quayside (Wp.21 113M). We retrace our steps up **Quay Street**, through **St Thomas's Square**, with a choice of 'eateries', to return to the Bus Station (Wp.1 120M).

26. St George's Down and Newport

Hidden in the 1930's suburbs of **Newport** is a Roman villa, not well known like its Brading cousin, but nonetheless a fascinating gem of Roman history - no crowds of tourists here. After our Roman interlude, we visit **Shide Quarry Nature Reserve**, another secret treasure, before setting off over the lower slopes of **St George's Down** on little-used and scenic footpaths. A gentle return over a pleasing landscape finishes with a 'secret' waterside path to the bustle of **Newport**.

Short Walk: From Wp.17 follow the track as it bends left, passing **Garretts Farm** on a footpath. At a road, cross onto a track opposite, turning left at a crossroads of tracks (Wp.30), to re-join the route (1 hour 45 mins, 4.5 miles/7.2 km).

Access by bus: Any bus to **Newport** Bus Station.
Access by car: Roadside parking in the vicinity of **Newport Roman Villa**, **Cypress Road**, start the walk from the Villa (Wp.6).

From the Bus Station (Wp.1 0M), we initially head towards the terminus entrance road, before turning right to pass round the library (Wp.2 1M). We diagonally cross **Church Litten Green**, stepping over the low wall at the far corner maintaining direction to cross the road by the traffic lights (Wp.3 3M) and turn left. At **Medina Avenue** we bear right (Wp.4 4M), following the **Roman Villa** sign, and take the third turning on the right, **Cypress Road** (Wp.5 7M), to visit the **Roman Villa** (Wp.6 9M).

Dated to around 270AD, one of eight found on the Island, the Villa would

Roman Villa

have belonged to a rich farmer, with a state-of-the-art bath house attached, four pools - from very hot, to cold. When the Romans left Britain, the main source of income disappeared - no legions to be fed, and the Villa gradually fell into disrepair until it was re-discovered in 1926.

Leaving the Villa, re-tracing our steps to the T-junction (Wp.5), we turn right, passing a luxury car showroom to turn left along **Shide Path** (Wp.7 11M). In 70m we turn left (Wp.8 12M), crossing an attractive wooden bridge over the **River Medina**, keeping ahead to cross a busy road (Wp.9 12M), and taking the rising road signed 'Pan, St Georges Down' up the right verge. At the T-junction with **Burnt House Lane**, we cross, up steps, to enter **Shide Quarry** (Wp.10 13M) - a chalk pit in use until WWII, and now a remarkable nature reserve. Dropping down a flight of steps to circle around the large quarry floor,

River Medina

with buzzards patrolling the cliffs, we leave the way we came, noting the old railway tunnel below to the right - now a bat refuge.

Shide Quarry

Exiting the quarry, we turn right, keeping ahead at a T-junction along **Pan Lane**, and, as the road bends left, we keep right, up a concrete ramp (Wp.11 25M) leading onto a track. Bearing right through a wooden barrier, a shady footpath leads us up to a road, which we cross to join a footpath (Wp.12 29M), soon emerging into a field. Turning right, we climb to the corner to enjoy fine views over the quarry and **Newport** (Wp.13 30M). Continuing round the field edge, passing a mystery watchtower, we climb the lower slopes of **St George's Down**, following the left fence line, with increasingly pleasing views to our right.

At **St George's Lane** (Wp.14 37M), we turn left, uphill, keeping to the right of a golf club car park along a wide track. By an occasionally muddy right hand lay-by (Wp.15 42M), we turn left, crossing stiles either side of a quarry road onto an attractive footpath, passing between ponds and emerging onto a golf course. Checking left for tee-offs, we cross straight over two fairways, making for a marker post below gorse bushes (Wp.16 45M), and turning right onto a track for 30m, before turning left over a stile. We turn right, down a track, passing **Garretts Farm**, and keeping ahead as the track bends left (Wp.17 46M), along a strip of terraced lawn through a charming garden. Passing through a field gate on a faint path through newly planted trees,

looking West from St George's Lane

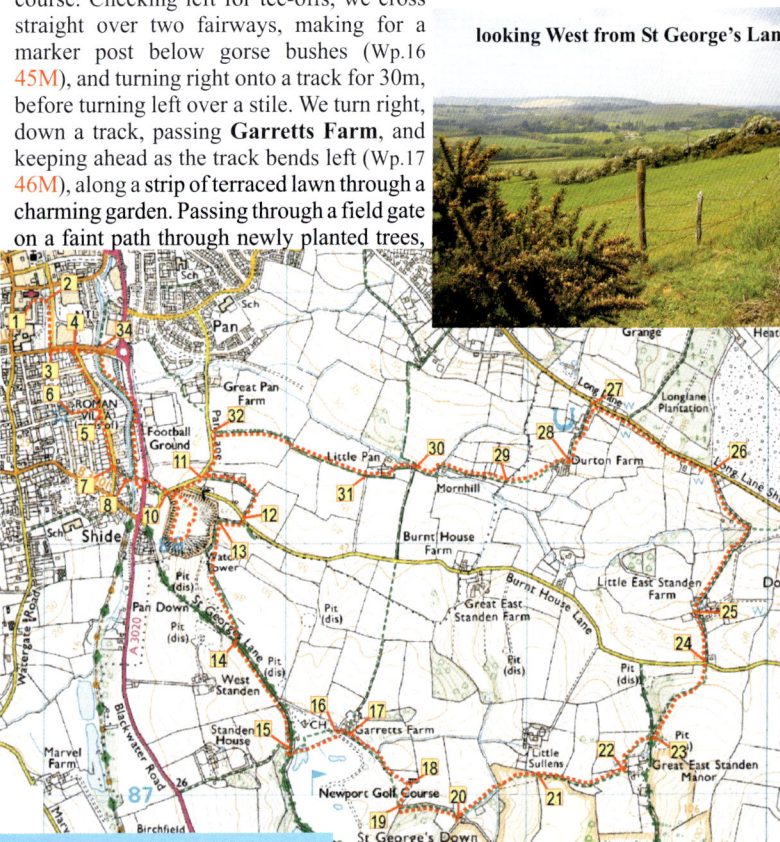

we re-join the golf course, crossing a track, and keeping to the right of a shallow ditch to descend to a warning bell. Carefully crossing two fairways, passing to the left of a bunker, we turn right along a wood edge (Wp.18 52M) before turning left over a stile (Wp.19 53M), onto a lovely woodland path.

After a stile, we pass along the bottom edge of a field, and cross over the hedge line, now keeping right down a short slope to turn left at the bottom (Wp.20 56M). We climb over a stile to join a gently descending path, crossing a bridge at the valley bottom, which leads us over another stile. We climb up the hillside on an invisible path, ultimately aiming to cross a stile in the far corner (Wp.21 62M). Through light scrub, on a rising path, we emerge to pass up the left fence line of a meadow, crossing another stile, and then dropping through light woodland. The next stile takes us into a field, and we head down diagonally to cross another stile in the far left corner (Wp.22 68M), to the left of **Great East Standen Manor**, before turning left and following the right fence line uphill to a corner post. We veer right, descending, making for a stile to the left of a cottage at the valley bottom (Wp.23 70M). Crossing, we turn left on an access road, and in 30m fork right, up a wonderful rising woodland path, awash with bluebells in May.

Emerging over a stile, we keep ahead across the top of a stand of trees, before veering left, downhill, over a stile which appears in the hedge, in line with a track dropping down the opposite hillside (Wp.24 76M). Crossing a road, we climb the track, passing **Little East Standen Farm** (Wp.25 80M), and keeping ahead on the main rising track, which eventually meets a busy road (Wp.26 88M).

We turn left along **Long Lane Shute**, taking extreme care (high visibility waistcoat recommended). The road climbs over a hill, descending to a dip just after **Long Lane Cottage**, where we turn left on an access track on footpath A50 (Wp.27 95M). Dropping through a pleasing landscape to **Durton Farm** entrance, we keep right on a fence-enclosed footpath (Wp.28 98M), negotiating a stile and diagonally crossing a field with a pond, to cross another stile in the far corner (Wp.29 103M). Keeping left, we pass two derelict caravans, and proceed, over a stile, into a miniature pony paddock. We pass through a ramshackle smallholding farmyard, and leave through a field gate on an access track.

sheep shearing

Passing through another gate, we keep ahead on the track, which winds its way over a crossroads (Wp.30 110M), and passes round **Little Pan Farmhouse**. At the end of a garden wall (Wp.31 113M), we keep ahead on a lovely path between fields. Cresting a rise, **Newport** appears ahead, as we descend to turn left up a lane (Wp.32 121M), soon joining our outbound route, and turning right opposite **Shide Quarry** entrance (Wp.10 124M). We descend to cross the busy road onto the footpath, turning right before the wooden bridge on the mill stream path (Wp.33 126M) which 'smuggles' us into **Newport**. Just before the road bridge (Wp.34 133M), we fork right climbing to join the road, turning left to cross the junction with **Medina Avenue** and return to the Bus Station (Wp.1 137M), or sample the delights of **Newport**.

27. Whitwell, Week Down and The Undercliff

Whitwell, a real village with a shop, Post Office and pub, is the start for this cracking walk. A meandering series of footpaths takes us through **Stenbury Manor** up to **Stenbury Down** and along the panoramic ridge crossing **Week Down**, before descending towards the Channel. We delve into the **Undercliff**, passing along one of the Island's unique paths at the base of the sandstone cliffs, then along a spectacular grass path above **St Lawrence**. Turning inland on the pilgrims' path, we pass through the superb **Dean Farm** to return over meadows to the **White Horse** pub.

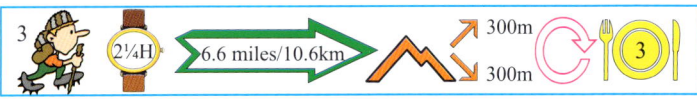

3 | 2¼H | 6.6 miles/10.6km | 300m / 300m | 3

Access by bus: No.6 to **Whitwell Chapel**.
Access by car: Roadside parking in **Nettlecombe Lane**, alongside Chapel.

We go up **Nettlecombe Lane**, alongside the Chapel (Wp.1 0M), passing through a railway bridge, with the old **Whitwell Station** up a slope to the left (now a private residence, but still looking the part). At a T-junction at the top of the Lane, we turn left through a bridleway gate (Wp.2 7M), passing a barn on a rising farm track. We keep ahead through a field gate, and in 50m turn left over a double stile footbridge (Wp.3 11M). We immediately turn right on GL54a, following the right hedge line down a meadow, crossing a stile and keeping ahead, with **Stenbury Manor** through the trees to our right. Crossing a shallow valley, we rise to pass a fingerpost and go over a nearby stile, turning right (Wp.4 17M). We follow the right fence around three sides of a meadow (Wp.5 18M), crossing a stile and footbridge, and then turn right down a track (Wp.6 19M), to pass the handsome stone built **Stenbury Manor** and farm.

Stenbury Manor

Maintaining direction on a rising track, soon between fences, we pass through a field gate by a fingerpost, bearing left on GL53 (Wp.7 24M) to cross a nearby stile up the slope to the left. Bearing left, we follow the left fence, rising to cross a stile in the corner, then dropping to a track (Wp.8 28M) and turning right for 30m before turning left over a stile. We follow the wind-tortured trees along the right bank, with fine westerly views, to a fence corner, and cross a field aiming for the right side of a fine stone cottage. Dropping to a sunken track, we turn right (Wp.9 35M), climbing past a stone barn, and keeping ahead, with tantalizing glimpses across the Island through the trees on our left.

Turning right at a marker post T-junction (Wp.10 42M), we climb sharply, passing through a bridleway gate, first following the left meadow hedge line, then the remains of a stone wall - once the boundary wall of **Appuldurcombe Park**. The steep, sometimes muddy, bridleway passes up and around the top of a disused pit, before emerging into a meadow, where we keep left to go through a corner bridleway gate (Wp.11 49M). Bearing half right, we diagonally cross the hillside pasture on an invisible path, contouring along the slope for economy of effort, and making for and crossing a distant stile 2/3 of the way up the hill in the fence line ahead (Wp.12 55M).

the stile up the hill

We follow a path, which veers slightly left, gently climbing to converge with the hedge above, and cross a hard-to-spot stile by a fingerpost (Wp.13 58M). Turning right, along a hedge and fence flanked bridleway on the ridge of **Week Down**, with lovely views both sides, we pass through a field gate (Wp.14 62M), and immediately turn left through a bridleway gate, before turning right to continue along the ridge. Passing through another bridleway gate by a fingerpost, on V38, a fine grassy path takes us past several round barrows in the field to our right, and then through a field gate, as we start our long descent towards the English Channel.

The track becomes hedge lined, as we ignore all turnings, dropping to the road, crossing and turning left (Wp.15 83M). In 25m we turn right, up steps, immediately turning right again on a path above the **Undercliff**, paralleling the road above. By a double fingerpost, we fork left, down V73 (Wp.16 85M), with occasional glimpses of the sea below, as we traverse down the **Undercliff**. Levelling out, with the cliff face revealed, we bear right at a fingerpost (Wp.17 90M), crossing a nearby stile, and climbing a twisty series of steps to a fabulous, adventurous path, along the base of the creamy sandstone cliffs.

As a flight of stone steps crosses our path (Wp.18 94M), we keep right, climbing to a T-junction and turning left. As our path turns inland (Wp.19 97M), we skirt around **St Lawrence Shute**, passing though a gate, and down steps, to cross the road (Wp.20 98M), and climb up the opposite side to cross a stile. Turning left, we continue along the top of the **Undercliff**, above **St Lawrence**, on a superb grassy path with tremendous coastal views. We cross a stile descending to a fingerpost crossroads (Wp.21 106M), turning right on V80 - **St Rhadegunds Path**, the route taken by Medieval pilgrims to visit the **White Well** (see Walk 37).

Sandstone Cliff path

The grass path rises, to cross a stile, keeping ahead down a tarmac lane, which somewhat destroys the illusion of walking in the pilgrims' footsteps. Descending to a road, we cross (Wp.22 112M), turning right along the verge, passing the charming farmhouse and turning left by a fingerpost on V116 (Wp.23 113M). Passing through **Dean Farm**, one of the finest stone built

a superb grassy path

farms on the Island, with some of the buildings now being utilised as Yates Brewery, we turn left through a field gate at the top, noting the ice-house and well, which serve the brewery, to the right.

We follow the main farm track along the meadow for 50m, then fork right (Wp.24 114M), on a slightly sunken grass track, which gradually rises to a stile (Wp.25 116M). Crossing, we stride straight down the middle of the meadow, making for, and crossing a stile to the right of a small stone barn (Wp.26 120M). We bear left, passing between fascinating stone cottages to go through a field gate to a fingerpost, and turn left on NT13 (Wp.27 122M). Passing through bridleway gates either side of the old railway embankment, we keep right, over the adjacent double stile bridge (Wp.28 124M), and diagonally cross a meadow to pass over a stile and footbridge spanning the infant **River Yar**. We go between cottages, turning right at the road (Wp.29 128M) to pass the **White Horse**, built 1454, and one of the oldest inns on the Island, to return to the **Whitwell Chapel** bus stops (Wp.1 130M).

rainbow over the barn

28. Appuldurcombe

From the tourist honeypot of **Godshill**, we meander through wood and field to climb **Gat Cliff**, crossing **Appuldurcombe** and **Stenbury Downs**, with superb all round views. Descending, we pass the magnificent **Appuldurcombe House**, and go through the massive **Freemantle Gate** - a reminder of the glorious past of the Estate. A fine undulating track, once used by visitors to the house, takes us back to **Godshill**.

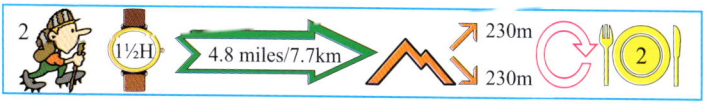

2 | 1½H | 4.8 miles/7.7km | 230m / 230m | 2

Access by bus: No.3 to **The Griffin**, **Godshill**.
Access by car: Public car park opposite **The Griffin**.

The Griffin & Godshill

We go up **Hollow Lane**, alongside **The Griffin** (Wp.1 0M), soon bearing left by a fingerpost (Wp.2 1M) and emerging to pass up a grassy valley. Going through a gate (Wp.3 6M), we keep ahead, following the valley bottom through an atmospheric wood, before crossing a plank bridge, and keeping right up a winding path to go through a gate (Wp.4 8M), turning right between fences. Passing attractive farm buildings, a track joins from the left, and we keep ahead on a pleasingly elevated path, turning left at a road (Wp.5 13M). Just after cresting a rise, we turn left by a fingerpost on GL59 (Wp.6 14M), crossing a stile to go up an access track.

We keep ahead, to the far end, through a selection of shotgun firing ranges, where we rise briefly into woodland, turning right by a gate (Wp.7 18M) and following a high deer fence up two sides of a large field. At the top, we turn left at a T-junction (Wp.8

climbing to the T-junction

26M), passing through a gate to a fingerpost crossroads, and then turning right on GL58 (Wp.9 27M). In 20m we pass between a stone wall and a fence, on a path that rises steeply to climb two flights of steps up **Gat Cliff**, with astonishing long views from the top.

We continue ahead, between fences, crossing **Appuldurcombe Down**, before climbing more steps to pass a fingerpost (Wp.10 42M), with **Wroxall** straggling along the valley below. We join an access road by a cattle grid, and bear left (Wp.11 49M), to enjoy westerly sea views across **Whitwell** and **Niton** villages, as we walk the heights of **Stenbury Down**. Descending from

the radio station, we turn left through a bridleway gate (Wp.12 53M), just before a fingerpost on our right, and then follow the left fence sharply downhill, passing through a gate and down steps to an access road (Wp.13 56M). We turn left, downhill, then left again at a road T-junction (Wp.14 62M). As the road bears right, we keep ahead on a track by a fingerpost on GL47, passing the very attractive **Span Lodge**, passing to the right side of a gate to join the footpath.

Appulldurcombe House

This lovely open path takes us through a bridleway gate, along the lower slopes of **Stenbury Down**, to track the vintage iron fence (Wp.15 73M), and then a wall, around the perimeter of the impressive **Appuldurcombe House**.

Replacing a Tudor house, the magnificent Baroque style mansion was built in 1701, with Capability Brown landscaping added later. From late Victorian times the house was largely uninhabited, although it was used by troops from both World Wars. The dilapidated buildings were finished off by a WWII land mine, to leave the House much as it is today, though it has been re-roofed in recent times.

Freemantle Gate

Crossing a stile, we pass over an access road to a fingerpost, and bear right on GL47 (Wp.16 77M), a rising track. The track, with sufficient height to please the discerning view collector, takes us through the 'triumphal arch' of **Freemantle Gate** (Wp.17 84M) - a struggle to close the hernia inducing wrought iron gate! We keep ahead along a lovely undulating track, through a patchwork of woodland and fields, to join the main road (Wp.18 96M), where we turn left to return to **The Griffin** (Wp.1 99M).

29. Mersley and Arreton Downs

From the **White Lion Inn** at **Arreton**, we cross a rich agricultural landscape, and drop through a pretty valley, before joining the **Bembridge Trail** to **Knighton** (pronounced K-nighton locally). We climb for panoramic views as we cross **Mersley Down**, and then **Arreton Down**, on a delightful access land path, accompanied in August by multitudes of butterflies. We return to the Inn past the beautiful **Arreton Church**.

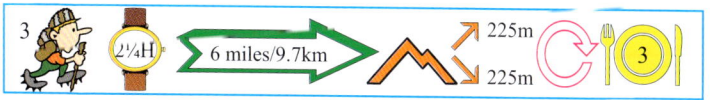

Access by bus: No.8 to the **White Lion Inn**, **Arreton**.
Access by car: Roadside verge opposite the **White Lion**.

Facing the **White Lion** (Wp.1 0M), we turn right along the footway towards **Sandown**, before turning right again, opposite a fingerpost (Wp.2 1M), and crossing the road up a track, A5b, between arable fields. At the top of the gently rising slope, with fine views ahead, we cross a stile (Wp.3 6M), before turning half left, steeply downhill, to make for and cross a stile and plank bridge at the corner of the wood in the valley bottom below (the fields here popular with clouded yellow butterflies in August). Passing up the left side of a wood, we turn left by a fingerpost (Wp.4 8M), to follow the top edge of the trees on a fine grassy track, which leads us through first one field gate and then another (Wp.5 13M).

Bearing slightly left, we drop to cross a plank bridge in the open field, keeping left to climb up to a fingerpost at the top of the slope and go over a stile (Wp.6 16M). Following the right hedge line to the busy road (Wp.7 19M), we cross, turning left, then right by the fine

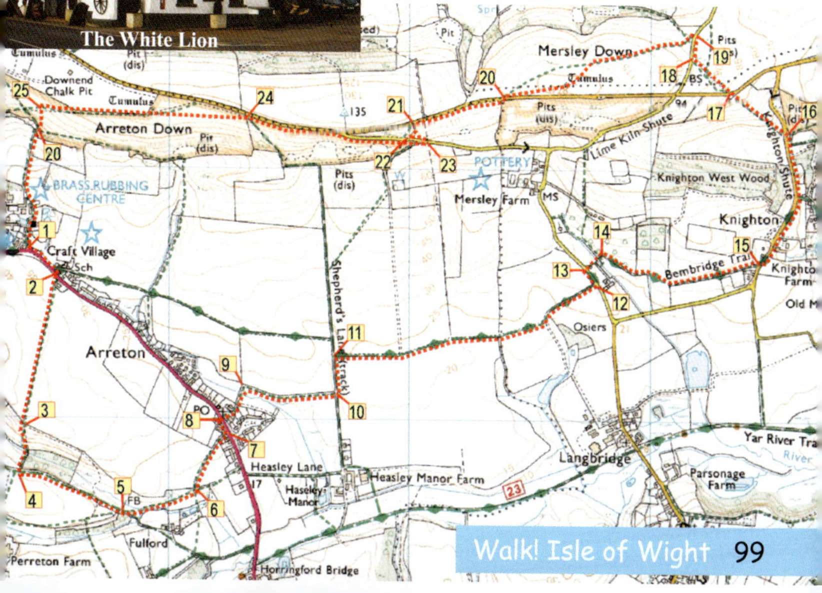

The White Lion

Victorian Methodist Chapel, on footpath A10 (Wp.8 20M). A gravel track takes us right, then left, to pass down the left side of a field and over a double stile footbridge (Wp.9 21M). We turn right, along a narrow meadow, crossing a stile in the far left corner and keeping ahead to turn left on a wide sandy track, **Shepherds Lane** (Wp.10 25M). At a track T-junction by a fingerpost (Wp.11 27M), we turn right, joining the **Bembridge Trail**, with the eastern Downs stretching away ahead, and **Newchurch** on the hill to our right.

the eastern Downs from Bembridge Trail

Keeping ahead, ignoring all crossing paths, we turn left at a road (Wp.12 42M), and in 60m turn right by a fingerpost on NC1 (Wp.13 43M). The undulating track soon climbs past a fingerpost (Wp.14 44M), curving right onto a grassy track leading into a field, as we follow the right hedge line. A few steps take us across a stile, along another field edge to a road, where we carefully turn left up **Knighton Shute** (Wp.15 53M). 35m after passing a fingerpost on our right, we turn left over a stile by a concealed fingerpost (Wp.16 62M), and then half right for a stiff climb up a meadow to the top of the hill, making for and crossing a stile beneath gnarled trees.

We emerge at a busy road (Wp.17 67M), crossing to go over a stile, and then through a meadow in the direction indicated by a fingerpost. Crossing the next stile (Wp.18 71M), we turn right, down the road, and then left by a fingerpost over a stile on R16 (Wp.19 72M). A near invisible path takes us across **Mersley Down**, below the crest, with fine panoramic views, before we drop gently towards the far left corner, going over a stile by a fingerpost in the left fence line (Wp.20 83M). Carefully crossing the busy road, we turn right, on a safe footpath below, paralleling the road. At a fingerpost, we turn left over a stile onto A16 (Wp.21 88M) - a charming shady path, and then turn right on a track to a road (Wp.22 90M). We turn left, downhill, and then hard right to climb the awkward, sloping access fence behind a fingerpost (Wp.23 91M) to enter the access land. A delightful winding path, takes us up and through disused pits, very loosely paralleling the fence above, as we go along **Arreton Down**.

In early August the amazing mating frenzy of thousands of chalkhill blue butterflies across the Down, presented the unforgettable experience of walking through 'butterfly clouds'.

'Chalkhill Blues'

We rise towards a fingerpost at the road edge, and pass through a steel gate to cross a stile on the left (Wp.24 101M), before dropping to a path along the Down, and gradually diverging from the road above. Passing along the edge of dense scrub, we bear left, just after going under power lines (Wp.25 111M), to make for an information board and the steps behind (Wp.26 113M). Descending the steps, we drop to pass a barn of the **Arreton Barns** tourist complex, and the beautiful **Arreton Church** with its rare early Norman stained glass window, before emerging at the road by the **White Lion Inn** (Wp.1 118M).

It takes but a few minutes to leave the summer hubbub of **Godshill** behind, to find peace and solitude on this lovely walk. A pretty wooded valley starts us off on the gentle climb around the flanks of **Appuldurcombe Down**, circling the summit to visit the **Obelisk** - a spectacular viewpoint, before descending to pass through the fascinating Donkey Sanctuary. We climb again, on mainly grass paths, over **St Martin's Down**, and up to **Shanklin Down**, with wonderful views across **Sandown Bay** as we descend to sample the delights of **Old Shanklin** village.

Access by bus: No.2 or 3 to **The Griffin** pub, **Godshill**.
Access by car: Car park opposite **The Griffin** pub, **Godshill**, bus back.

We go up **Hollow Lane**, alongside **The Griffin** (Wp.1 0M), and in 40m bear left by a fingerpost on GL57 (Wp.2 1M), emerging to pass up a grassy valley. Going through a kissing gate (Wp.3 7M), we keep ahead, following the valley bottom through an atmospheric wood. We cross a plank bridge, keeping right up a winding path to go through a bridleway gate (Wp.4 10M), and then turn right between fences. As we pass a stone built farm, we turn hard left up GL58 (Wp.5 13M), soon crossing a stile to gently climb a track.

the terraced track

Passing over a dip in our track, we go through a gate and over two stiles, passing a four-way fingerpost (Wp.6 23M), and in 25m **turn right over a gated stile onto a permissive path.** Following the farm track, we pass through a gate, along the bottom of a pasture and through another gate. As the track opens out into a meadow (Wp.7 31M), we bear left, climbing a sheep path up to a T-junction with a track (Wp.8 33M), beyond which lies a disused pit. We turn right, up the beautiful terraced track, with fine views west, and go through a gate (Wp.9 38M). Following the right hedge line up, we pass some round barrows, with **Sandown Bay** coming into view as we cross a stile near the top (Wp.10 43M).

the Obelisk

rim of the disused pit

Turning left on GL58, we descend to a fingerpost (Wp.11 49M), bearing half right over a stile, and heading for the **Obelisk** (Wp.12 54M), with spectacular views across the Island. The **Obelisk** is a memorial to Sir Robert Worsley, of **Appuldurcombe House**, erected by Sir Richard Worsley in 1747, and restored by another Sir Richard Worsley in 1983.

Turning right, we descend, curving around the rim of a disused pit, and down a sunken rocky path, which drops down the steep open hillside to a fingerpost and stile in the wall below (Wp.13 61M). Crossing, we turn right, on a lovely path, passing through a bridleway gate, and following a boundary wall of **Appuldurcombe Estate**, with **St Martin's Down** looming above **Wroxall**. At the slope bottom, with the magnificent **Freemantle Gate** to our right, we keep ahead over a bridleway crossroads, through a bridleway gate. We go through three more gates, cross a road onto the opposite bridleway (Wp.14 70M), and pass through another two gates before going through a final bridleway gate in a dip (Wp.15 75M). Bearing right, and soon descending to cross a plank bridge, we continue into the fascinating **Donkey Sanctuary**.

inmate of the Donkey Sanctuary

We pass through, keeping ahead to leave by a field gate, to join a gently rising, sunken, hedge-enclosed track. At a road (Wp.16 80M), we carefully cross, turning right, then left, up an access

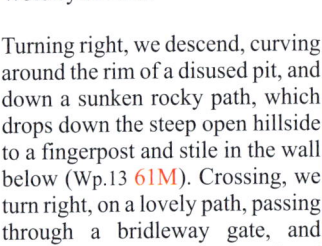

road on NC43. Keeping ahead, we cross a stile by a field gate, passing up a small meadow, and over a stile to cross the tree-enclosed course of the old railway line. A climbing woodland path emerges through a gate into a meadow, as we head towards the distant **St Martin's Down**. We cross a stile in a fence which appears ahead, maintaining direction over two more meadows. Going through a footpath gate, we immediately cross a stile (Wp.17 92M), circling around the right side of a boggy area, to make for and climb a stile in a fence visible on the hillside ahead.

Maintaining direction to the far right meadow corner, we cross a stile, continuing to a nearby fingerpost and turn right (Wp.18 96M), soon passing another fingerpost onto V46. A delightful sunken path rises through mature beech and plane trees, emerging through a bridleway gate. We keep ahead, up V46, to cross a meadow, and pass through a gate and up the edge of a large disused pit (Wp.19 105M). Following the cattle track, which bears left to the upper slopes of **St Martin's Down**, we join a wide grass path, climbing towards **Shanklin Down**. Bearing right by a fingerpost (Wp.20 111M), we follow the left fence line up, and, just over the brow of the hill, turn left over a stile (Wp.21 113M). Passing over the summit of **Shanklin Down**, we enjoy fabulous views over **Sandown Bay**, as we maintain direction on our descent toward **Shanklin**.

Old Shanklin village

At the bottom corner, we bear left between fences, turning right by a fingerpost and crossing a stile on SS10 (Wp.22 120M). Our path passes along the top of a wooded cliff, crossing a stile, down steps, and dropping delightfully, as we keep ahead ignoring all crossing paths. We encounter more steps and another stile, before passing diagonally down two arable fields, and crossing yet another stile to step over a wall into a churchyard (Wp.23 132M). Passing the attractive church, we cross an access road, passing a duck pond, to walk down a park green, loosely paralleling the main road. At the far right corner (Wp.24 136M), we join the road footway into **Old Shanklin** Village for refreshments, before catching the bus back (Wp.25 141M).

The Village Inn is the pick of the pubs. It sells a bitter called 'Village Idiot'. When lazy holidaymaker husbands send their wives to the bar for a pint of bitter, they invariably, with a smug grin, return to their slothful spouses with a pint of 'Idiot'!

31. Wooton Old Mill Pond and Havenstreet.

A varied walk, which visits two pubs and four substantial woodlands - the ancient **Hurst Copse**, **Combley Great Wood**, **Kemphill Moor Copse** and **Firestone Copse**. The section between **Combley Farm** and the steam railway line is delightful, gaining enough height to give satisfying views as we cross a charming, mainly livestock farming, landscape. The highlight is undoubtedly the waterside path in **Firestone Copse**, through gnarled and twisted oak trees alongside the banks of the **Old Mill Pond**.

Access by bus: No.9 to the **Sloop Inn**, **Wooton Bridge**.
Access by car: The **Sloop Inn** car park, with permission.

From the westbound bus stop (Wp.1 0M), facing the **Sloop Inn**, we turn left and take the next left up an access road (Wp.2 1M), invitingly signed 'Woodland Burial Grounds'! At a fork (Wp.3 3M), we bear left on a stony track, between buildings of **Fernhill Farm**, soon passing through a bridleway

Hurst Copse boardwalk

gate. As the track bends left, we turn left (Wp.4 8M), crossing a stile into the ancient woodland and nature reserve of **Hurst Copse**. Following a stunning path through the wood, we cross a fine boardwalk (Wp.5 10M) through a reed bed on the west edge of the **Old Mill Pond**. Turning away from the water, our path takes us through elm trees, now largely wiped out by disease on the mainland, to cross a stile opposite **Fernhill Ice House** (18th C), where we turn left (Wp.6 13M), rejoining the stony track as it climbs a slope.

Keeping left at a T-junction (Wp.7 19M), we follow the main track as it winds through woodland and field to cross the **Isle of Wight Steam Railway** line (Wp.8 23M). Going through a gate, we pass **Woodhouse Farm**, with its small wooden old granary at the top of the slope on the left, as our main track meanders to a T-junction where we turn left onto bridleway N15 (Wp.9 30M). The track takes us round **Great Bridlesford Farmhouse**, with its attractive duck pond. Leaving the farm through the middle gate of three (Wp.10 35M), on a grassy track, we pass through two more gates, as we keep to the main track, which emerges at a busy road (Wp.11 40M).

Crossing, we turn right, and in 30 metres duck through a post and rail fence behind the bus stop, onto a narrow woodland path just inside **Combley Great Wood**. After crossing two ditches (Wp.12 42M), we bear right through fir trees to a T-junction of paths (Wp.13 43M), where we turn right. At the next T-junction (Wp.14 47M) we turn right again, and in 30m hard left, onto a stony forest track, gently undulating through the woods to a T-junction (Wp.15 53M) where we turn right on another track. Fifty metres after our track bends sharply left, we bear right onto a fine woodland path (Wp.16 55M), leaving the main track, to pass up through an eerily quiet pine wood. Ignoring an offset crossing path, we keep ahead, winding through a delightful bluebell-rich coppice. At a T-junction with a track (Wp.17 62M), we turn right, and then cross a stile by a half barrier gate. As our path curves right, crossing a track to a house, we bear left down a woodland path (Wp.18 64M), following the left garden fence line.

Emerging through a bridleway gate, we keep left across the top of a meadow,

Combley Farm

enjoying fine views across the valley, before bearing half right to pass through a field gate in the bottom far corner (Wp.19 71M), then turning right down a farm track. We keep ahead, passing through the very attractive **Combley Farm**, leaving on the main track (Wp.20 74M), which bears right. At a dip in the track before a cattle grid, we turn hard left, through a wooden bridleway gate (Wp.21 76M), diagonally crossing a meadow to the top left corner and passing through a field gate. Turning left, following the left hedge line along a meadow, we go through another gate and meadow, cutting off the left corner to pass through two adjacent field gates in the hedge line ahead (Wp.22 85M).

We cross straight over an arable field, leaving through a gate, keeping ahead along a farm access road. The main track swings right descending (Wp.23 90M), passing through a gate, skirting the edge of **Duxmore Farm**, then keeping right, up a substantial track, which undulates between several fields, with enough height to yield pleasing views. Going through a footpath gate (Wp.24 97M), we turn left, passing **Little Duxmore**, and immediately turn right on a rising access track, which continues to a road (Wp.25 103M).

Turning left, then right, through a field gate by a fingerpost on R22, we cross a meadow in the indicated direction, with **Ashey Down** ahead. Passing through a field gate by a lone ash tree (Wp.26 105M), we bear left to very loosely follow the left fence line, on an invisible path down a large meadow. We pass through a gate by an electricity pole, tracking the left hedge line, then cross a gap, swapping sides to follow the right hedge down to cross the steam railway through gates (Wp.27 116M). Going over a small field and a concrete bridge,

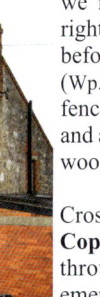

White Hart Inn

we maintain direction to the top right meadow corner, turning left before a fingerpost and gate on R19 (Wp.28 120M). We follow the right fence down, over a plank bridge, and around the field to a stile at the wood edge (Wp.29 123M).

Crossing into **Kemphill Moor Copse**, we take the main path through the impressive wood, emerging over a footbridge stile and crossing a field to go over another stile in the far left corner (Wp.30 134M). Turning right at the road, we then take the next left, **Pondcast Lane** (Wp.31 136M), passing **Pondcast Farm** and winding up to a road T-junction (Wp.32 143M), where we turn left into **Havenstreet**. Passing the church, we continue to another T-junction, opposite the **White Hart Inn** (Wp.33 146M), where we turn right, and then left by a phone box (Wp.34 148M) on a footpath down a gravel track.

As the track bears right, we drop, to follow the left fence, and eventually descend to cross a stile at the valley bottom (Wp.35 154M). Turning left, over another stile, we cross a stile footbridge into **Firestone Copse**, keeping

the waterside path

ahead over a crossing path. We continue up, passing to the left of a car park, to a junction of tracks (Wp.36 158M). Turning hard left, signed **Wooton Creek Trail**, we follow the wide track down bearing right (Wp.37 162M), following the main track round until, at a sharp right bend, we turn left (Wp.38 171M), by a yellow footprint into a handsome pine wood, with glimpses of the **Old Mill Pond** reed bed appearing below. We descend to skirt the bank - an outstanding waterside path through twisted oak trees, before taking the upper path by a yellow banded post, to skirt around a boggy inlet (Wp.39 175M), soon regaining the waterside path by another post.

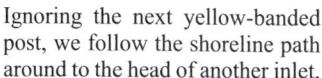
another section of the waterside path

view across the pond

Ignoring the next yellow-banded post, we follow the shoreline path around to the head of another inlet, then away from the water (Wp.40 184M), before bearing left to cross a valley bottom and climbing up the other side to a junction of paths (Wp.41 185M). We turn right, with the wood edge just visible through the trees to our left, and follow the obvious gently rising path. As the main path veers right, downhill, we keep ahead, weaving through the trees to emerge at a road near the top left corner of the wood. Turning left (Wp.42 189M) brings us to the main road (Wp.43 194M), where we turn left again to return to the **Sloop Inn** (Wp.1 197M).

32. The White Well, St Lawrence, Ventnor and Luccombe

Whitwell was named after the **Holy White Well**, a place of pilgrimage in Medieval times. Pilgrims arriving by ship would climb **St Rhadegund's Path**, devout in belief of the healing properties of its waters. The church consists of two separate chapels, now joined as one. **St Rhadegund's** was built in the 12th century, and **St Mary's** in the 13th century. The cynic in me suspects that **St Mary's** was built to 'cash in' on the pilgrim trade.

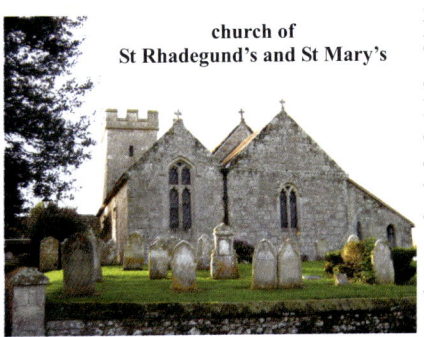
church of St Rhadegund's and St Mary's

Starting from **Whitwell Church**, we follow in the pilgrims' footsteps, and wind our way down through **St Lawrence** to join the Coastal Path. A fine trail takes us above quiet coves, before we slip inland to visit the semi-tropical, and very impressive, **Ventnor Botanic Gardens**. Returning to the **Coastal Path**, we undulate over headlands, to pass the **Spyglass Inn**, and along the seafront of **Ventnor**. Easy walking on the sea wall defences, below the cliffs, takes us all the way to **Bonchurch**, with the beautiful **St Boniface Church**. The **Coastal Path** weaves its way through the fascinating **Landslip** to **Luccombe**, where we climb inland, passing a fine farmhouse and up to the main road bus stops.

Short Walks:
(a) **Whitwell** to **Ventnor**. Follow the route to Wp.23, turning left into the town centre for the bus at **Ventnor** (Boots). (1hour 35mins, 4.4 miles/7.1km)
(b) **Ventnor** to **Luccombe**. No.3 or 6 bus to the town centre bus stop, **Ventnor** (Boots). Go down to the sea front, turn left to commence the walk at Wp.23 (1hours 5mins, 3.1 miles/5km)

Access by bus: No.6 to **Whitwell Church**.
Access by car: Roadside parking near **Whitwell Church**, bus back.

From the **Ventnor** bound bus stop (Wp.1 0M), we start by following the **Pilgrims'Path** up the road for 60m, before turning left down a grassy path, NT15 (Wp.2 1M), to actually pass the recently re-discovered **Holy White Well**. Having been denied access to the curative waters by a grill, we continue down, crossing a stream before bearing right to pass through a steel gate next to a stile (Wp.3 5M). We cross the old railway embankment, emerging through another gate, and proceed up a meadow, to turn right at a fingerpost on NT12 (Wp.4 7M). The track passes between fine stone cottages, and we cross a stile next to a stone barn (Wp.5 9M), passing up the middle of a long narrow pasture, and crossing another stile by a steel gate (Wp.6 15M). A faint grass track curves left, downhill, to go through a steel gate (Wp.7 18M), as we turn right, passing through the yard of the beautiful, stone built, **Dean Farm**, now put to alternative use as Yates Brewery.

At the road we turn right, along the verge, soon turning left up a tree lined access road (Wp.8 20M), **St Rhadegund's Path**. Crossing a stile at the summit, we drop over a field towards the sea, passing a four-way fingerpost (Wp.9 28M) to a viewpoint, with an amazing view over **St Lawrence** and **The Undercliff** - part of the largest single area of landslip in Western Europe.

We descend sharply, through a kissing gate, and down steps, traversing the secondary cliff on a fine path to emerge at a road (Wp.10 32M). Crossing into **Seven Sisters Close**, we keep ahead onto a footpath as the road bears right, descending to another road (Wp.11 34M). We cross, turning left, then right (Wp.12 35M), down **Old Pond Road**, before turning left (Wp.13 37M) into **Wolverton Road**. By a fingerpost (Wp.14 39M), we turn right, on V97, passing through a kissing gate, steeply down, and keeping left to cross a stile. Following the right fence line to a fingerpost (Wp.15 42M), we turn left, joining the **Coastal Path**, and cross a stile by a gate. We turn right on a track (Wp.16 44M), which narrows to a hedge enclosed path, before opening out as a fine cliff top path above **Woody Bay** (Wp.17 45M).

the Coastal Path

The path takes us above deserted coves to keep ahead up a concrete slope into a meadow (Wp.18 66M), and in 20m we bear left, down to **Ventnor Botanical Gardens**, passing round the back of a play park (Wp.19 68M). There are various routes through the gardens, with differing themes. Whichever paths you choose, the ultimate aim on reaching the eastern end is to turn right (Wp.20 73M), up towards the sea, to re-join the **Coastal Path** and turn left towards **Ventnor**.

Ventnor Botanical Gardens

Turning right, back on ourselves (Wp.21 75M), we go down concrete steps, passing through **Steephill Cove**, with its seafood bars and kiosks. Keeping

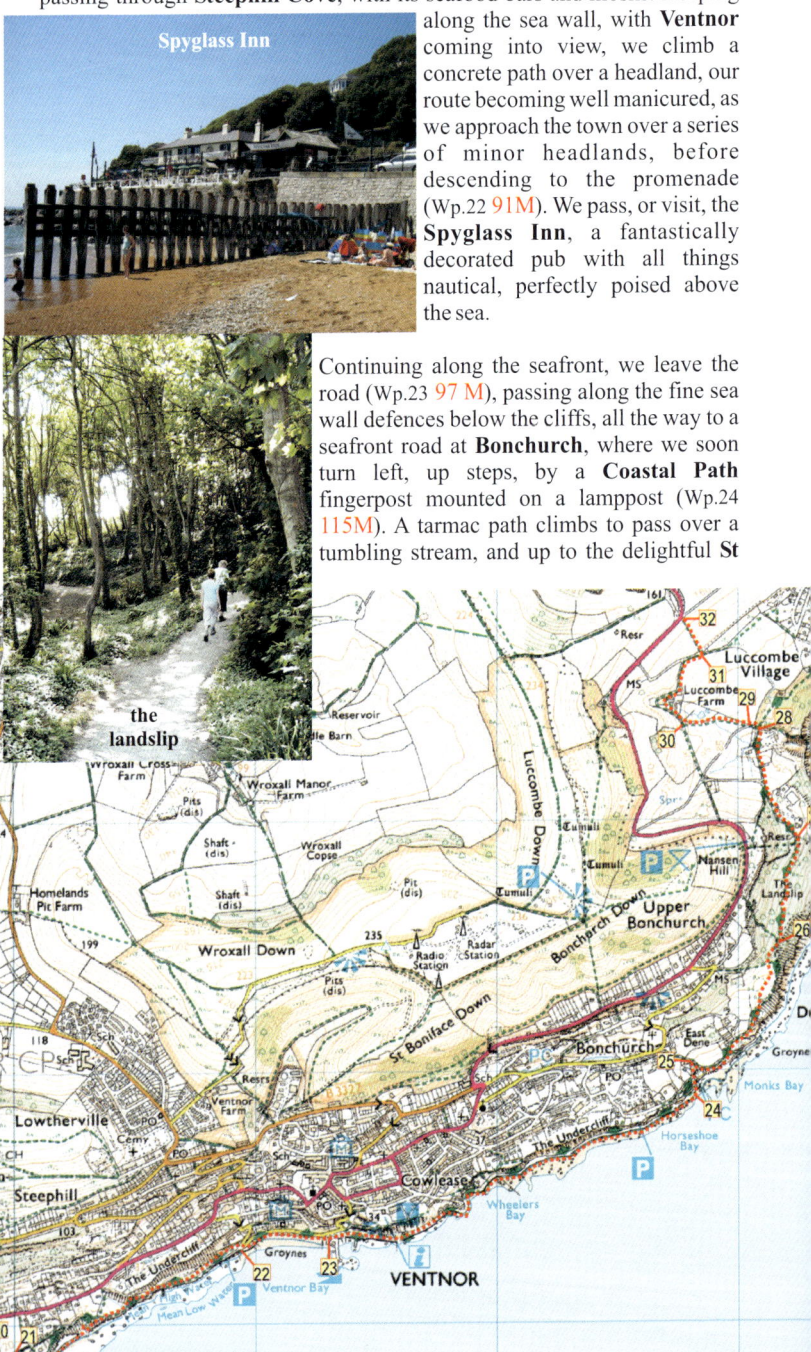

Spyglass Inn

along the sea wall, with **Ventnor** coming into view, we climb a concrete path over a headland, our route becoming well manicured, as we approach the town over a series of minor headlands, before descending to the promenade (Wp.22 91M). We pass, or visit, the **Spyglass Inn**, a fantastically decorated pub with all things nautical, perfectly poised above the sea.

Continuing along the seafront, we leave the road (Wp.23 97 M), passing along the fine sea wall defences below the cliffs, all the way to a seafront road at **Bonchurch**, where we soon turn left, up steps, by a **Coastal Path** fingerpost mounted on a lamppost (Wp.24 115M). A tarmac path climbs to pass over a tumbling stream, and up to the delightful **St**

the landslip

Boniface Church, an Island treasure. By the church, we turn right on V69 (Wp.25 117M), to follow the **Coastal Path** along the cliff top above **Monks Bay**. We meander through the undulating **Landslip**, negotiating stiles, gates and bridges, keeping to the main **Coastal Path** (Wp.26 134M), and ignoring all others.

We finally emerge at a T-junction with a drive (Wp.27 143M), where we turn left, and soon after our first glimpse of **Sandown Bay**, keep ahead at a fork of tracks, down a wide path passing along a driveway. Keeping to the left of a row of iron posts, we follow a concrete access road curving left (Wp.28 151M), and then soon turn right to cross a stile by a fingerpost (Wp.29 152M). We go up a meadow to the top left corner, bearing left over a stream, following the right fence line uphill. Crossing two stiles in the corner (Wp.30 156M), we turn right on a farm track, go through a gate, and pass around the picturesque **Luccombe Farm** on a concrete access road.

up the slope to the stile

The road climbs, and as it swings sharply left, we keep ahead on a grass track, crossing a stile by a gate. In 50m we fork left, up a slope, to cross a stile by a fingerpost (Wp.31 160M), and then turn sharp left, by-passing an overgrown stile, to follow the right fence line steeply uphill. At the top, we go up steps to cross a stile, emerging at the main road and bus stops for the return journey (Wp.32 162M).

33. Wroxall Horseshoe and America Wood

A wonderful walk around this exceptional area. We gently climb the slopes to **Wroxall Down**, circling the **Horseshoe** on beautiful paths, with superb views across **Wroxall** to **Stenbury Down** beyond. Continuing over **Luccombe** and **Shanklin Downs**, looking across **Sandown Bay**, before we descend a quirky flight of steps, and move on through one of the finest woodlands on the Island - **America Wood**. Returning over the flanks of **St Martin's Down**, to the unspoilt village of **Wroxall**, which has a charm of its own, we finish at the friendly **Four Seasons Inn**.

3 | 2½H | 7 miles/11.3km | 330m / 330m | 4

Short Walk: Wroxall Horseshoe. Follow the route to Wp.8, turning left on the bridleway above the steep slope, passing below a disued pit to re-join the route at Wp.20, keeping ahead by the bridleway gate. (1 hour 35 mins, 4.5 miles/7.2km)

Access by bus: No.3 to the **Four Seasons Inn**, **Wroxall**.
Access by car: Roadside parking up **Manor Road**, by the **Four Seasons Inn**.

We go up **Manor Road**, alongside the Inn (Wp.1 0M), bearing right up **Stenbury View**, and keeping ahead by a fingerpost up V15 - a hedged bridleway of great antiquity. Passing through a bridleway gate (Wp.2 10M), we keep ahead, climbing sharply before opening out to a field, and following the left hedge as we ascend **Wroxall Down**. Through another gate, we rise to

across the Horseshoe from Wroxall Down

pass a nearby fingerpost, where we bear left on V4. Soon after, at a fork of two clear paths (Wp.3 18M), we keep left, initially gently uphill and directly towards a distant radio mast on the horizon.

We follow the wide grassy main path around the **Horseshoe**, along the slopes of **Wroxall Down**, our path rising to parallel the radar station fence, and eventually joining the car park access road (Wp.4 35M). In 35m, we turn left through a kissing gate, following the main path on **Bonchurch Down**, which continues to circle around the **Horseshoe**, and along the heather clad flanks of **Luccombe Down**. With several round barrows visible on the skyline to our right, our path joins a substantial stony track (Wp.5 42M), close to a barrow, and passes along the ridge of **Luccombe Down**, with views across **Sandown Bay**

cattle on Bonchurch Down

appearing.

Passing through a bridleway gate to a fingerpost, we turn right on SS9a (Wp.6 51M), and in 20m, left on SS11, soon crossing a stile to follow the left hedge along **Shanklin Down**. We have the option to enjoy the panoramic view across the Bay from the trig point, before we turn left (Wp.7 56M), over an adjacent stile, and then right along a track to re-join the fine view across the **Horseshoe**. Following the right fence down, passing a fingerpost, we drop through trees, and down another field to turn right, over a stile by a fingerpost on SS10 (Wp.8 63M). In 20m, we bear left over another stile, descending an amazing zig-zag flight of steps, down the inland cliff face.

the Horseshoe from Luccombe Down

looking across Sandown Bay

At the foot of the steps, we bear half left, crossing a double stile in the fence below (Wp.9 67M), and retaining stunning views, as we cross a field to go over a stile, which appears in the fence ahead. We descend steeply to the far right corner of the next field, crossing a double stile onto a hedged path (Wp.10 73M). Over another stile, we pass across the course of the old railway line, keeping ahead down a drive to the main road (Wp.11 78M). Crossing carefully, we turn right to a nearby fingerpost, and then left on NC37a, down steps on the stunning woodland path to **America Wood** - perhaps the most attractive woodland path on the Island.

America Wood

At a double marker post, by a wooden barrier (Wp.12 88M), we turn hard left on a path through bracken, and in 80m, at a T-junction (Wp.13 89M), we turn left on a wide descending path. Turning right at a footpath marker post (Wp.14 90M), we drop to cross a nearby stile, emerging on the obvious path to cross first a stile, and then a footbridge, before bearing left into a delightful meadow. We head for the far right corner, up a flight of steps (Wp.15 94M) to cross a stile and turn left at a road. Passing the tastefully converted **Apse Manor Farm**, we turn right by a fingerpost on NC32 (Wp.16 97M), up a farm track, keeping ahead into the nearby field corner to diagonally cross the very large arable field.

At the far side, we cross a footbridge (Wp.17 102M), turning left along a sometimes shady, sometimes open track, until we cross a road onto NC31

(Wp.18 110M). Passing over an old railway bridge, with the track bed in a deep cutting below, we go through a bridleway gate into a field, following the left hedge on a lovely curving path up the hillside. Going through another bridleway gate on a fenced path, gently climbing the slopes of **St Martin's Down**, we keep ahead, passing two fingerposts (Wp.19 121M), onto a fabulous climbing track, through mature beech and plane trees, with glimpses across **Sandown Bay**.

We emerge through a bridleway gate to turn hard right (Wp.20 124M), and follow the right fence, before crossing a stile to pass along the obvious woodland edge path. Bypassing, or climbing, another stile takes us into a meadow, to follow the right hedge, past the mystery site of **Cooks Castle**. We continue around the meadow on a fine grass path down to the bottom corner (Wp.21 131M), crossing a stile and bearing right twixt fence and hedge, towards **Wroxall**. We descend, high above a bridleway below on our right, eventually crossing a stile and joining a road down into the village. We bear right near the bottom, over the old railway bridge, turning left at the main road by the church (Wp.22 139M). Passing the **Worsley** pub, we go through the village, a charming unspoilt place, with a post office and a village shop – no tourist trap here, to return to the recommended **Four Seasons Inn** (Wp.1 143M).

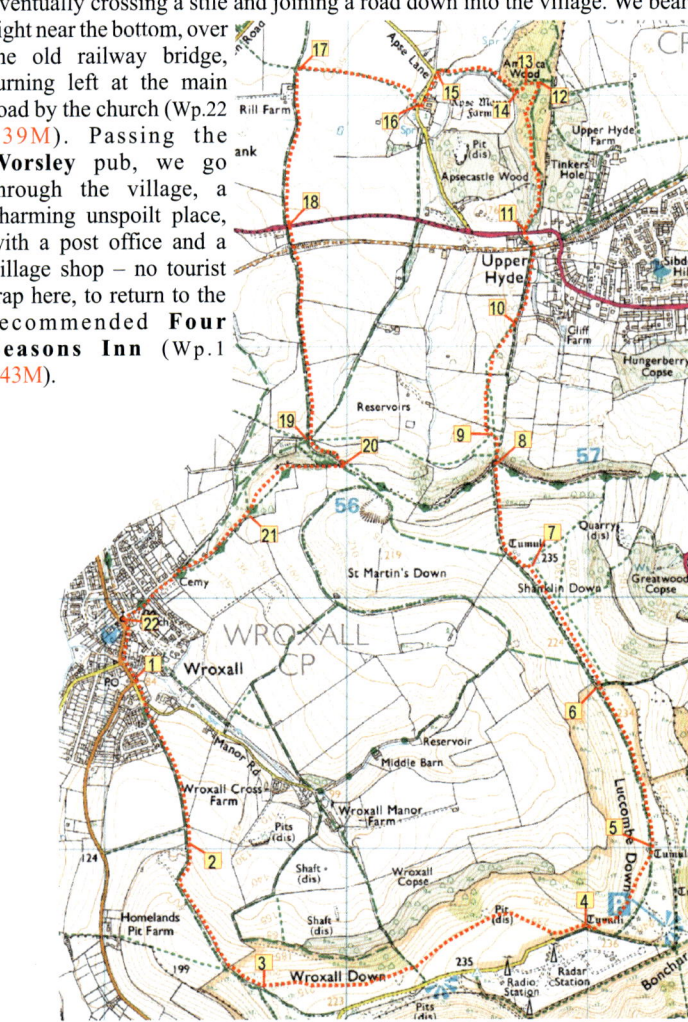

34. Quarr Abbey

From the attractive **Old Mill Pond** and harbour setting of **Wooton Bridge**, we head for **Firestone Copse**, passing through this fine, varied, woodland on a winding path. We visit the War Memorial on a lonely hill near **Havenstreet**, before going through a lovely copse by a lake on our route to the ruins of the Medieval **Quarr Abbey**. Passing through the grounds of the new **Benedictine Abbey**, we join the **Coastal Path** to return to the **Sloop Inn** at **Wooton Bridge**.

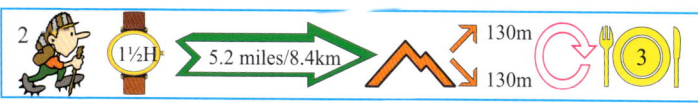

2 · 1½H · 5.2 miles/8.4km · 130m / 130m · 3

Access by bus: No.4 or 9 to the **Sloop Inn**, **Wooton Bridge**.
Access by car: Car park in front of the **Sloop Inn**

From the **Sloop Inn** (Wp.1 0M), we head across the **Causeway** on the right footway, climbing the hill and turning right, up **Firestone Copse Road** (Wp.2 4M). As the road drops to the fringe of **Firestone Copse**, we turn left by a road sign (Wp.3 10M), on a winding woodland track of varying width, weaving through fine trees and coppicing, with the left edge of the wood always in sight.

Passing through a half barrier gate, we turn right at a road (Wp.4 18M), and in 20m left, down a woodland path, before gently rising through coppicing to a T-junction with a woodland track (Wp.5 21M). We turn left toward the wood edge, and in 30m bear right onto a lovely path, loosely paralleling the nearby left wood edge. Keeping left at a fork of paths (Wp.6 24M) near the next field corner, and winding close to the wood edge again on a superb pinewood path, we make our way to one wood corner (Wp.7 26M), then another, and another by a ditch (Wp.8 28M). We turn right, following the ditch away from the corner, to a T-junction with a wide forest track. We turn right, and in 30m left, then immediately bear right on a pine needle carpeted path, following the top edge of the pine plantation.

We keep ahead, descending gently, as the wood edge comes into view again, and our path becomes a little overgrown before emerging at a road, where we turn left (Wp.9 35M). At the top of the hill, we turn left again by a fingerpost (Wp.10 39M), crossing a stile, and proceeding up a meadow to visit the First World War Memorial at the hill top, with far reaching views. Crossing a nearby stile, we descend a narrow field, and go over another stile, keeping ahead to pass through a nearby field gate. A right

Firestone Copse pine needle path

hedge line leads us to another gate and through **Newnham Farm**, with its timber clad granary, to a road where we keep ahead (Wp.11 49M).

As the road bears right, we turn left, crossing a stile by a fingerpost on R4 (Wp.12 52M). A lovely path down a meadow, takes us to the valley bottom, where we cross a stile by a stunning lake to pass through **Puckers Copse**. Crossing a stile (Wp.13 59M), we bear left over a pasture to the far left corner, going over another stile, and then crossing the main road (Wp.14 61M), to pass down the track opposite. At a track T-junction with the **Coastal Path** (Wp.15 64M), we turn right to view what we can of the remains of the Medieval **Quarr Abbey** from the field entrance, and the bench seat beyond.

The Abbey was originally founded in 1132, and dismantled in 1536 (Dissolution of the Monasteries) - the stone being used by Henry VIII for building castles at East and West Cowes, and at Yarmouth (the only one left standing). The remaining ruins are incorporated into **Old Abbey Farm**, with some surviving sections of walls and outbuildings scattered around the surrounding fields and woods.

Retracing our steps, we head west on the wide stony **Coastal Path** track, turning right at a crossroads (Wp.16 68M), on the tarmac access road to the 'new' **Quarr Abbey** - built in 1914, and considered to be a masterpiece of brickwork, (but actually reminds me of a building from a Noddy book!). A Benedictine house for a community of displaced French monks, you may enter the Abbey and join one of the services if you so desire.

'new' Quarr Abbey

Bearing left in front of the Abbey (Wp.17 71M), a concrete road takes us through the monks' livestock paddocks of pigs, sheep and goats, to join the **Coastal Path**, where we turn right at a junction of tracks (Wp.18 73M). We eventually emerge at a road by the **Fishbourne Inn** (Wp.19 79M), turning left, to pass the car ferry entrance, and then right by a fingerpost and telephone box (Wp.20 83M). We descend, turning left at the bottom (Wp.21 84M), keeping ahead at a crossroads onto a stony track, and soon passing between steel barriers into a wood to cross a bridge. We keep ahead up to the main road (Wp.22 90M), turning right to return over the **Causeway**, perhaps for refreshment at the **Sloop Inn** (Wp.1 96M), with its fine garden overlooking the harbour.

Surprisingly quickly, we leave the bustle of **Sandown** behind, soon joining the old **Newport** to **Sandown** railway line through the wetlands of the eastern **River Yar** and **Alverstone Meads Nature Reserve**. We climb for a pleasant interlude through beautiful woodland and on to **Newchurch**, with the option to visit the **Pointer Inn**. Rejoining the trackbed, with the river alongside, we branch off at **Horringford**, going cross country through meadow, wood and valley, and finally crossing fields to the **White Lion Inn** at **Arreton**.

Access by bus: No.2, 3 or 8 to **The Heights**, **Sandown**. Return on No.8 from **Arreton**.
Access by car: Roadside parking in side roads near **The Heights**.

From the bus stop (Wp.1 0M) we walk towards **Sandown**, turning left into **The Heights** car park (Wp.2 1M) and making for the far right corner to join the 'Los Altos Park and Trim Trail'. We bear right at a fork (Wp.3 2M), up a rising path, before descending steps onto an open hillside, and heading downhill to the bottom right corner (Wp.4 4M). Bearing right, through the park, we loosely parallel the railway line, turning left at a gate, under the railway (Wp.5 8M).

We go over a zebra crossing (Wp.6 9M) onto a playing field, turning half right to loosely follow the right fence line, and eventually join a road, where we keep ahead between playing fields. After passing a golf club entrance, we turn

Highland Bull at Alverstone Mead

left by a telegraph pole fingerpost (Wp.7 16M), and in 50m go through a gate, turning right to pass through a kissing gate. We drop down steps, to cross a footbridge through a wetland wood, before proceeding along a boardwalk, and across another footbridge to reach a T-junction with the old **Newport** to **Sandown** railway line (Wp.8 18M). We turn left along the cycleway - a fine, open trackbed route, with **Brading** and **Ashey Downs** to our right, and pass through the wetland nature reserve of **Alverstone Mead** (perhaps with Highland Cattle grazing alongside).

Crossing the road at **Alverstone** (Wp.9 33M), we continue our railway trip to a fingerpost (Wp.10 37M), where we turn left over a footbridge and then continue up, to pass through a kissing gate into a meadow. Climbing the slope we go through another kissing gate (Wp.11 39M), bearing left, uphill, on a fabulous high woodland track, awash with foxgloves in early summer, and passing through two kissing gates, with tantalizing glimpses of the surrounding countryside through the trees. As the track swings left, we turn hard right by a fingerpost (Wp.12 45M), crossing a stile and dropping sharply down another superb woodland path.

dropping steeply down

At a marker post by a gate (Wp.13 47M), we turn left, to cross a sleeper bridge, and follow the right fence uphill. Turning left at the top (Wp.14 50M), we gently climb towards **Newchurch**, and, as the track enters woodland, we turn left again (Wp.15 53M) to pass along the length of the well 'populated' graveyard. Passing the shamefully laid flat gravestones into the open grassy churchyard, we make for the far right corner (Wp.16 56M), with the option of turning left to visit the 600 year old **Pointer Inn**, or continuing the walk by turning right down the steps.

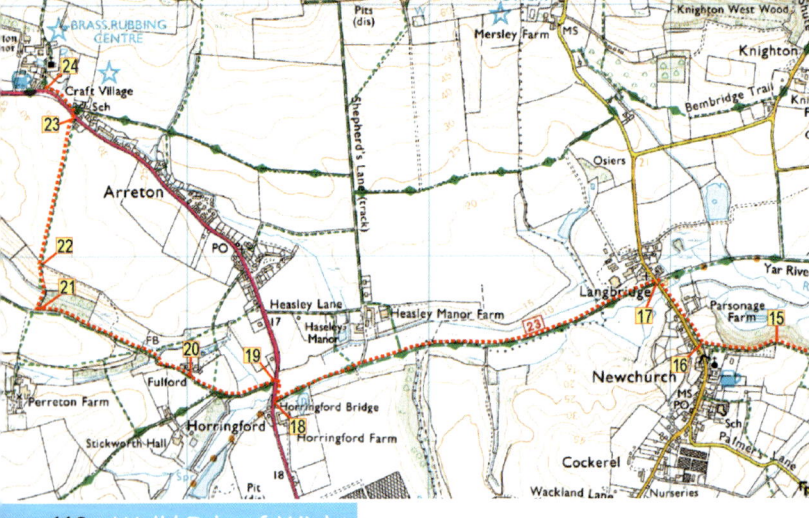

At the bottom of the steps, we turn left, down a shady track, paralleling the road below. On joining the road, we keep ahead, descending to cross a stone bridge, and turning left to re-join the old railway trackbed cycleway (Wp.17 60M). Continuing, we eventually pass the attractive **Heasley Manor**, and then turn right at the road at **Horringford** (Wp.18 77M). Crossing the bridge, we go over a pedestrian crossing onto bridleway A2 (Wp.19 78M), and as the cycleway swings left by a white gate, we keep ahead, up a farm track. We soon fork right, rising to pass a fingerpost.

the terraced grass track

As the track bends right towards a house, we turn left through a bridleway gate (Wp.20 81M), diagonally crossing a field to go through another gate in the corner. The path descends through two further gates and a small wood to the bottom, where we turn left, climbing above a tree-hidden stream to pass through a field gate. Keeping ahead on a lovely terraced grass track, we gently rise to pass through another gate, and alongside a wood. At the end of the wood, we turn right by a fingerpost (Wp.21 89M), dropping to go over a bridge stile at the valley bottom. Turning half left, we traverse up the steep hillside to cross a stile, which appears in the fence line at the top (Wp.22 92M). An open farm track between fields gently descends to the main road (Wp.23 98M), and we turn left to the bus stops, or **Arreton** and the **White Lion Inn** (Wp.24 100M).

Arreton Church

36. Bonchurch Challenge and The Devil's Chimney

The challenge is a 640 foot climb, guaranteed to stimulate heart, lungs and legs, up steps and the very steep hillside of **Bonchurch Down** - the highest point on the Island. From **Bonchurch Shute**, we go down into the Victorian churchyard and pass through the charming, picturesque village, to climb **One Hundred and One Steps**, then the **Chimney Steps**, and finally scale **Bonchurch Down**. We are rewarded with superb views across the **Wroxall Horseshoe**, which we cross on some charming paths, often accompanied by Highland Cattle, before climbing to **Luccombe Down** for more breathtaking views. Descending **Nansen Hill**, overlooking the Channel, we join the lovely **Parapet Walk** to the top of the **Devil's Chimney**. Swallowed up by Lucifer's jaws, we are disgorged into **The Landslip**, on delightful, meandering, undulating paths through the undergrowth and trees. We return to the superb **St Boniface Church** - a real gem, and get the chance to sup at what many consider to be the finest pub on the Island, the **Bonchurch Inn**.

4 | 2¼ H | 5.8 miles/9.3km | 440m / 440m | 5

Short Walk: Just **Bonchurch**. Turn right at Wp.8, along the footpath behind houses and paralleling the road, turning right at Wp.18, through a bridleway gate to re-join the route. (1 hour 10 mins, 3 miles/4.8km)

Access by bus: No.3 to **Upper Bonchurch** letter box, at the top of **Bonchurch Shute**.
Access by car: Roadside parking in **Bonchurch Shute** near **Bonchurch Inn**.

From the bus stop (Wp.1 0M), we wind down **Bonchurch Shute**, passing the entrance to **Bonchurch Inn**. Immediately after the T-junction with **The Pitts**,

Village pond

we go through a wrought iron gate (Wp.2 6M) on a lovely path, meandering down into the churchyard. Passing in front of the church, which is wholly Victorian, we turn left immediately after the main door, on a grass path which dives down a cutting, passing through a green door to an access road below (Wp.3 8M). Turning left, we then turn right at a road along the footway, to go through the charming village. We pass the **Huish Memorial Grotto** (c1868), a stone pyramid set in the wall (c1773), the Pond Stores and Post Office, and the picturesque pond, which is teeming with fish and wildlife.

Just before a red telephone box, we turn right on V106 (Wp.4 15M), up **One Hundred and One Steps** - the first phase of our 640 foot climb. At the top, the path bears right between walls, joining with a road. By a stumpy fingerpost, at the entrance to **Greycliff** (Wp.5 20M), we turn left up a gravel drive, to climb the second phase - the **Chimney Steps** (dating back to the 1700s), up through the cliff face.

Emerging at the top (Wp.6 25M), we turn left, high above Bonchurch, and in 50m, turn right (Wp.7 26M), crossing the road to go up a flight of steps on V108 (you may be tempted to think 'V' stands for vertical!). Passing through a kissing gate (Wp.8 27M), the final, and hardest part of our climb begins, with a flight of wooden steps followed by the very steep south face of **Bonchurch Down**. We go through another kissing gate, keeping ahead to a fingerpost (Wp.9 38M), and turn left on a narrow path through bracken, to join the car park access road passing alongside the radar station. As the road bends left, we keep ahead, passing between posts (Wp.10 42M), on a wide open grass path, which loosely parallels the nearby road, and affords superb views across the wonderful **Wroxall Horseshoe**, from the highest hill on the Island.

Passing brick pill boxes, we turn right by a fingerpost at the road edge (Wp.11 51M), descending with a fine view across **Wroxall** below. Going through a bridleway gate, we descend into a wood keeping ahead, emerging through another gate (Wp.12 56M), to follow the right fence down a meadow. We negotiate a field gate onto a descending farm track, and pass through **Wroxall Manor Farm**. The farm and surrounding areas are at the centre of wildlife conservation projects within the **Horseshoe**. Particularly interesting are the large number of Highland Cattle - impressive, but shy, beasts.

Leaving the farm and cottages, we turn hard right by a fingerpost on bridleway V2 (Wp.13 65M), up **Middle Barn Lane**. We pass the barn, climbing gently, to go through a bridleway gate, and up a sunken grassy track, V27, which winds delightfully up towards the Downs. Joining a farm track, we pass through a bridleway gate, to climb a field edge and go through another gate. We turn half right, by a fingerpost, on V28 (Wp.14 82M), up an invisible path, traversing up the hillside and heading for a fingerpost, which appears at the top (Wp.15 86M). With a long view across **Sandown Bay**, we bear right,

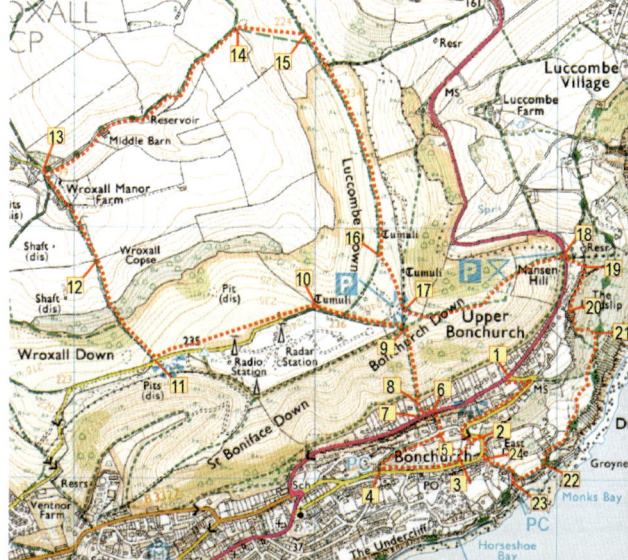

passing through two closely spaced bridleway gates, and keeping ahead along the top of **Luccombe Down**.

At a fork of paths (Wp.16 97M), by a heather clad barrow, we keep left on a stony track, passing the left edge of a car park before bearing half left (Wp.17 100M). The wide grass path gradually swings left to delightfully descend the ridge of **Nansen Hill**, with wonderful sea views. The obvious path passes through scrubby woodland and a clearing, then through a squeeze, as we drop down the hillside meadow to pass through a bridleway gate (Wp.18 110M). We cross the road, making for an information board in the far right corner of the car park, and descend to a wall (Wp.19 111M).

Turning right along the excellent, winding, **Parapet Walk**, perched on the cliff edge; we are safely constrained by a fine stone wall. Climbing a small flight of steps, we keep left along the bottom of a green of the **Smugglers**

emerging from the 'chimney'

top of double wooden staircase

Haven Tea Gardens, to go down some steps and turn right to re-join the **Parapet Walk**. We weave along to the top of the **Devil's Chimney** steps (Wp.20 114M), descending through the deep, dark, narrow cleft, and emerging into the fascinating world of **The Landslip**.

Turning right, we go down more steps, onto a winding path, before turning left up four steps and then descending to go down a double wooden staircase. A shady path takes us to a fingerpost T-junction, where we turn right (Wp.21 120M), joining the **Coastal Path** along the undulating, meandering path. Keeping ahead at a fingerpost, we go through a kissing gate, and pass a converted farm to join a descending access track. At the bottom, we turn right, up steps (Wp.22 129M), passing above the lovely **Monks Bay**, to a fork of paths where we keep left. At a tarmac path, we turn right (Wp.23 131M), climbing to visit the superb **St Boniface Church**, in its delightful setting.

Leaving the church, we bear left up a road, passing **East Dene** - childhood home of the Victorian poet Swinburne, and at a T-junction (Wp.24 134M), we turn right, to return up **Bonchuch Shute** (Wp.1 141M). An opportunity to visit **Bonchurch Inn** should not be missed - a genuine unspoilt pub, set in a converted coach house, with a unique atmosphere - a national treasure!

Old Bonchurch Church

Bonchurch Inn

37. Newchurch and Ashey Down

From **Newchurch**, delightful footpaths take us to briefly join the old railway line, before steadily climbing to pass along the flanks of **Ashey Down**, with fine **Solent** views, as we descend to visit the charming vision of an age gone by, **Ashey Station**, on the **Isle of Wight Steam Railway**. Turning back, we climb **Ashey Down** to the **Sea Mark**, descending to pass through the hamlet of **Knighton**, and joining the railway line to return to the 600 year old **Pointer Inn**.

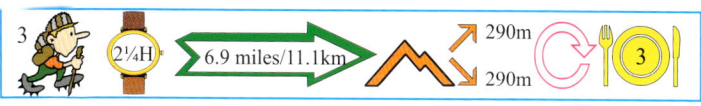

3   2¼H   6.9 miles/11.1km   290m / 290m   3

Short Walk:
Knighton circuit. Follow the route to Wp.10, keeping ahead along the road and turning left over a stile at Wp.19, as the road bends sharp right. (1 hour 35mins, 4.7 miles/7.6km)

Access by bus: Newchurch has a limited bus service. The options are Wightbus No.24, Southern Vectis No.21, and in summer the prolific Downs Tour open top bus from **Ryde**, every half hour. All services to the **Pointer Inn**.
Access by car: Roadside parking near the **Pointer Inn**.

From the bus stop (Wp.1 0M), we walk past the **Pointer Inn** and church, entering the open churchyard (sadly the gravestones have been laid flat at the rear), and follow the path to the far left corner (Wp.2 2M). We turn right, through the 'current' headstones - surprisingly well populated for a small village. At the end, we make for the far left corner (Wp.3 5M), exiting onto a track and turning right.

With fine views, the stony track takes us past a fingerpost to a steel gate, where we turn right (Wp.4 9M). We descend to cross a stream footbridge, and soon turn left through a gate (Wp.5 13M), on a delightful lightly wooded path. Passing through a kissing gate, we turn left up a rising woodland track, turning left again through the next kissing gate to drop over a meadow into trees. A

fine views as we climb

kissing gate and footbridge take us to the old railway line (Wp.6 22M), where we turn left, and immediately after crossing an iron bridge, we turn right through another kissing gate (Wp.7 24M).

Keeping ahead, passing a fingerpost on a twisty woodland path, which soon opens out, we climb between fences with fine views, and go over a fingerpost crossroads on NC5 (Wp.8 31M). After a long steady climb, we go through a bridleway gate, turning left at a road (Wp.9 43M), along the verge. Before reaching a telegraph pole, we turn right, crossing to go over a stile by a fingerpost (Wp.10 44M). Initially following the right hedge, then maintaining direction by a telegraph pole, we cross a shoulder of **Ashey Down**, passing a pair of medieval pillow mounds (thought to have been artificial rabbit warrens).

With the **Solent** coming into view, and a beautiful deep valley below to our right, we descend to cross a stile by a gate. Joining a track, and crossing another stile (Wp.11 54M), we then bear left down an access

the deep valley

steaming through Ashey Station

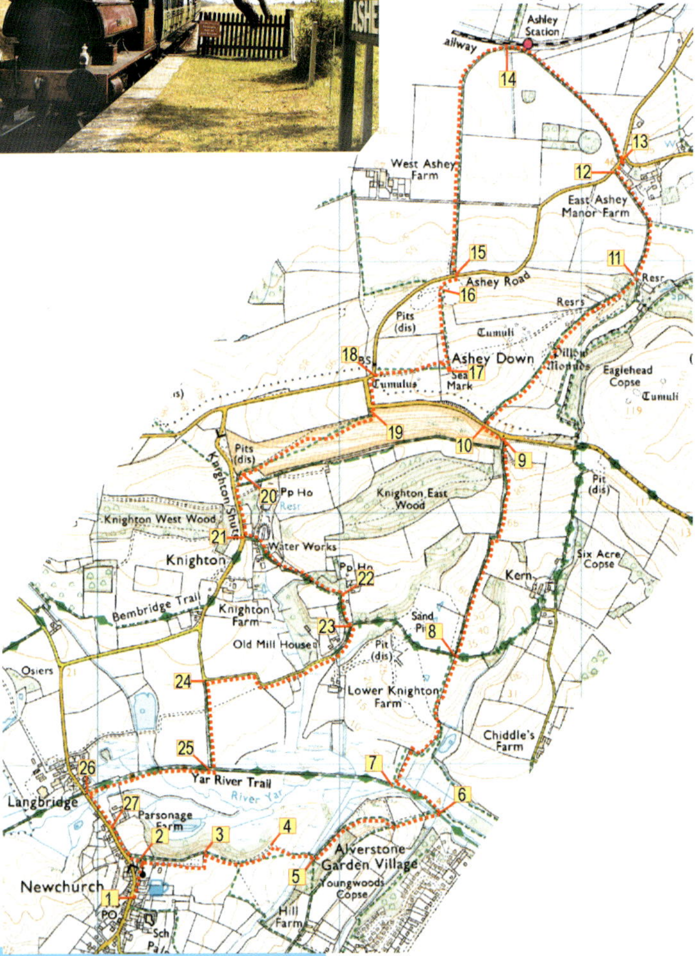

road. Passing a farm, we emerge at a road (Wp.12 58M), turning right, and in 40m, left on R29 (Wp.13 59M). The track takes us to **Ashey Station**, on the **Isle of Wight Steam Railway.** With careful timing you may be able to see trains steaming through - indeed, the platform is a top picnic spot.

We do not cross the line (Wp.14 65M), but keep ahead to cross a stile by a field gate, following the left hedge line as our path curves back towards **Ashey Down**. Crossing stiles either side of a farm access road, we go up a meadow edge to cross another stile, passing

Ashey Seamark

through a small wood, climbing up the bank and eventually crossing a stile onto a busy road (Wp.15 79M). We turn right, and in 30m cross, going over a stile, turning right again, before bearing left to climb flights of steps between chalk pits (Wp.16 80M). Keeping ahead, we climb **Ashey Down**, crossing a stile and making for the **Sea Mark** - built as a navigation aid in 1735.

From the **Sea Mark** (Wp.17 88M), we pass a nearby fingerpost, descending west, with stunning views, to cross a stile by another fingerpost, and turn left at a road (Wp.18 92M). Crossing a road T-junction, we immediately turn left along the verge, to follow the right fence to a fingerpost, and cross a stile onto footpath NC3 (Wp.19 94M). Initially heading downhill before bearing right, we gently traverse down the hillside to the top edge of a wood, towards the bottom left corner, seeking a stile, which appears in a vintage iron fence just inside the trees (Wp.20 103M). Crossing, we drop to the road, turning left down **Knighton Shute**, and at the bottom of the hill we turn left again, on NC45 (Wp.21 107M), soon bearing right to pass through the hamlet of **Knighton**.

Continuing on a rising stony track, we turn right, at a three-way junction (Wp.22 111M), downhill on a grassy track. At a T-junction, by a marker post (Wp.23 113M), we turn right, down a field edge, before bearing right again, along the access road from a sand pit, with the fine **Lower Knighton Farm** nearby. As the road bears sharp right, by a fingerpost, we turn left down NC53 (Wp.24 121M), before turning right again as we join the **Yar River Trail** along

Pointer Inn & Church

the old railway line (Wp.25 124M), which runs alongside the infant river. At a road, we turn left (Wp.26 130M), carefully crossing a bridge before forking left up a track after the entrance to **Parsonage Farm** on NC11 (Wp.27 132M), paralleling the road. As the track bears left, we turn right up a flight of steps into the churchyard (Wp.2 134M) to return to the 600 year old **Pointer Inn** (Wp.1 136M).

38. Brading Down and Bloodstone Copse

the Bull Ring & Wheatsheaf Inn

The **Brading Bull Ring**, now positioned outside the 'new' **Town Hall**, is a less than pleasant aspect of the past, last used in 1820. It is hard to believe that in Elizabethan times it was illegal to butcher a bull unless it had been baited!

From the **Bull Ring** we pass along the fine village **High Street** to visit the church. The Island was the last place to be converted to Christianity in England, and the church is thought to be the site of the first baptism in 687 - the beginning of the end for Island paganism. A fine, but little used, footpath takes us over fields and stiles and on through **Bloodstone** and **Eaglehead Copse** nature reserves. A beautiful path along **Brading Down** affords expansive views to the **Solent** and across **Sandown Bay** before we descend to the village, spoilt for choice on the refreshment front.

2 | 1½H | 4.3 miles/6.9km | 155m / 155m | 4*

*(The Snooty Fox)

Access by bus: No.3 to **Brading Bull Ring**, opposite the **Wheatsheaf Inn**.
Access by car: Village car park near the church, start from Wp.2.

From the **Bull Ring** (Wp.1 0M), we head down the attractive **High Street**,

storm clouds over the High Street

passing **The Bugle Inn** - the name deriving from a local dialect word for a young bull, and nothing whatsoever to do with musical instruments! Near the church entrance we encounter the old town lock-up and stocks, and in the churchyard, the town animal pound and gun shed, once used to house the parish gun! Inside the fine church is the impressive **Oglander Chapel**, the Island's most important historical family.

Leaving the church (Wp.2 4M), we cross the road, turning left, then first right, along **Cross Street** (Wp.3 5M), and bearing right again at a T-junction up a tarmac path. Emerging at a road junction (Wp.4 11M), we turn left along a sometimes busy road, passing the entrance to **Nunwell House**. We take another left just before a sharp left bend, up a flight of steps, on B23 (Wp.5 12M). Crossing a stile, with Nunwell nestling in the shallow valley to our left, we keep ahead across an arable field, passing to the left of a scattered line of oak trees to cross a stile (Wp.6 16M). Maintaining direction over a low hill on an 'invisible' path, we make for a stile and plank bridge at the base of a large oak tree. Still keeping ahead, we cross stiles either side of a farm access road by a fingerpost (Wp.7 23M), which we ignore as unrelated to our path, and maintain direction, crossing two fields and two stiles to enter a narrow, shady wood of tall mature trees (Wp.8 29M).

Nunwell House

At a T-junction of paths (Wp.9 31M), we bear left, then right along a field edge, re-entering woodland at the corner to wind through the eerie **Bloodstone Copse**. Legend has it that blood from a battle between Saxons and Danes, on nearby **Ashey Down**, flowed into the stream turning the stones red. At the next T-junction, by a fingerpost (Wp.10 35M), we bear left to wend our way through the nature reserve of **Eaglehead Copse**, emerging at a road (Wp.11 46M). Turning left, up the wide verge, we crest the brow of the hill with fine views across the **Solent** and **Sandown Bay**, before crossing the road to a small car park and passing through an access land gate next to a field gate (Wp.12 63M).

'Marbled White'

Brading Down

The delightful grass path takes us along **Brading Down**, with superb views to the **Yarborough Monument** on **Culver Down** ahead, round to the landslip

headland below **St Boniface Down**.

Passing to the left of an underground reservoir, we turn left through a bridleway gate by a fingerpost (Wp.13 82M), passing through a car park to cross a road onto an unmarked local path. Immediately turning right (Wp.14 83M), we initially parallel the road, before taking a left fork and crossing a chalky track. Our grassy path descends towards **Brading**, soon bearing left down a well-trodden path (Wp.15 84M), to a T-junction with a chalky bridleway (Wp.16 85M), where we turn right, downhill. As a corrugated fence appears, we turn left through a steel kissing gate (Wp.17 87M), before dropping down a meadow to pass through another kissing gate by a play park (Wp.18 89M). Turning right, then left at the nearby road (Wp.19 90M), returns us to the **Bull Ring** bus stop (Wp.1 93M), and a cream tea, or a pint!

After a pleasing meander over undulating farmland, a shady lane drops us onto the promenade at **Seagrove Bay**. Rounding **Horestone Point** takes us to a different world, the beautiful, isolated **Priory Bay** beach. A delightful coastal path, winding through lovely woodland along the low cliff top, brings us to the fascinating **St Helen's Old Church** tower before returning across **The Duver** and over the impressive **Old Mill Ponds** causeway for the return to **St Helen's Green.**

2 | 1¾H | 4.8 miles/7.7km | 150m / 150m | 2

Access by bus: No.9 bus to **St Helens**, **West Green** bus stop.

Access by car: Roadside parking outside the **Vine Inn**. Facing the Inn (Wp.10), turn left, passing the Post Office to join the walk at Wp.1 at the junction with **Field Lane**.

From the **Bembridge** bound bus stop (Wp.1 0M), we turn left down **Field Lane**, keeping left at a fork along **West Green** and following the narrow road round to the right. At the lane end we turn left onto a track, R77 (Wp.2 3M). Passing over a stile, we cross a pleasing shallow valley, loosely following the right hedge line. Over the next stile we turn right (Wp.3 6M), through a large arable field, crossing another stile, and then turning left along the tree lined **Attrill's Lane** (Wp.4 9M), with views across the **Solent** to **Portsmouth** and the **Spinaker Tower**.

At a junction of farm tracks (Wp.5 12M) we turn right, descending and curving right passing a spaced out cluster of fine oak trees at the valley bottom. As the track turns left and climbs towards a farm, we turn sharp right (Wp.6 16M), passing through a bridleway gate and soon climbing between post and rail fences. Going through an equestrian unit we pass to the right of a corrugated barn, briefly on a concrete farm road, before

joining a path on our left by a fingerpost. We pass a fingerpost junction, continuing ahead on R78 bridleway to a road junction where we turn right to pass the 'new' **St Helen's Church** (wisely built further inland than its predecessor, which was washed away by the sea in 1703!).

As the road turns sharp right, we go ahead through a kissing gate (Wp.7 25M), on footpath R80, crossing a large field and turning left at an unmarked T-

the walkway and steps

junction (Wp.8 28M). After crossing two stiles, we pass the road to **Priory Bay Hotel** (Wp.9 32M), dropping down a shady tarmac lane, following the **Coastal Path**, to almost unexpectedly emerge at the promenade at **Seagrove Bay** (Wp.10 40M). Turning right, along the prom, leads us up a fine wooden walkway and steps (Wp.11 44M) into a delightful winding woodland path along the low cliff top - the finest coastal path not on the **Coastal Path**!

Priory Bay beach

A short flight of steps drops us onto the beautiful, unspoilt sandy beach of **Priory Bay**, where we turn right along the shore. Passing the path up to the **Priory Bay Hotel** - lunch or a drink at the nearby **Oyster Bar** a possibility here in July and August - we continue to the end of the sea wall (beware of damp feet on a high spring tide), and turn right up a very steep flight of wooden steps (Wp.12 52M). We follow the fabulous path, winding along the low cliff top, with stunning glimpses across the Caribbean like beach and the **Solent**. After passing round **Node's Point**, we

old St Helen's church tower

emerge onto a sandy beach, turning right to pass **Old St Helen's Church** tower (Wp.13 81M), all that remains of the Saxon original.

The sea-facing side of the tower was clad in brickwork and painted white for use as a navigation mark by the Admiralty. In the eighteenth century **St Helen's Roads** was used as an anchorage by the Navy. Stones from the church ruins were used to scour the wooden decks, from which originates the expression 'holystoning'.

We continue along the sea wall, turning right, inland, immediately after the **Baywatch Beach Café** (Wp.14 83M), emerging through the scrub and turning left across **The Duver**, an area of consolidated grassy sand dunes. Loosely paralleling the road we eventually cross in front of the Hovertravel Engineering sheds, turning right by a fingerpost on footpath R86 (Wp.15 89M). Skirting along the harbour edge, we turn left across the **Old Mill Ponds** causeway (Wp.16 92M) and

the harbour edge

leave the harbour at a road junction (Wp.17 100M), turning right, uphill, to **St Helen's Green** (Wp.18 106M). We turn half left across the Green to pass, or visit, the **Vine Inn** (Wp.19 108M), before continuing past the Post Office and mini-roundabout to return to the **West Green** bus stop (Wp.1 111M).

40. Bembridge and Culver Down

Marvellous beaches, sand dunes, cliff tops, woodland, downland, marshland, harbour, a Victorian fort, and a windmill! Few walks have such a variety of landscape and interest. We start round the harbour mouth and **Bembridge Point**, beach walking to pass the **Lifeboat Station** and on to the **Crab and Lobster** to join the cliff top path up to **Culver Down**. The Victorian **Bembridge Fort** can, alas, only be viewed from the wrong side of the fence, but is none the less an impressive structure in a dominating position. Crossing the marshes brings us to the only surviving windmill on the Island, with a final shady section back to the start.

Note: Very high spring tides and stormy weather are to be avoided.

Access by bus: No.9 or 12 to the **Royal Spithead Hotel** bus stop, at the end of the **St Helens – Bembridge** causeway.
Access by car: Public car park near the **Royal Spithead Hotel**.

From the **Bembridge** bound bus stop (Wp.1 0M), we pass between iron posts

the eroding shoreline

towards the harbour beach, through the sand dunes, to walk on the beach past the harbour entrance (Wp.2 3M) and around **Bembridge Point** (Wp.3 4M). A degree of agility is required at times, as we continue along the beach, passing the tooth-like remnants of old sea defences on a shoreline which is slowly being eroded by the sea. The **Coastal Path** joins us, before we cross over the **Lifeboat Station** pier entrance (Wp.4 29M), descending a few steps to walk along a sea wall.

clifftop path looking towards Whitecliff Bay

As the **Coastal Path** disappears inland, we take to the beach, with fine **Solent** views, ships at anchor, and a fascinating beachscape of rocks, sand and shingle. Rounding the point, we climb a ramp (Wp.5 38M) to go along the sea wall, turning right by the **Cabin Café** (Wp.6 42M), away from the sea. Climbing steps, forking right to visit the famous **Crab and Lobster Inn** along the **Coastal Path**, or left to continue our walk, we emerge into a car park (Wp.7 43M), and turn left along the cliff top **Coastal Path**.

This section affords fine seascape views interspersed with delightful shady woodland, right through to **Culver Down**. At a T-junction of paths (Wp.8 55M), we turn left on a shady path, with **Whitecliff Bay** unexpectedly coming into view, our path soon weaving round a recent cliff slip. At the end of the Environmental Studies Centre fence (Wp.9 64M), we bear left, down steps, on an undulating shady path, emerging into a field by a holiday centre. The descending concrete path to the left gives us the option of visiting the beach, with its unique 2 to 90 million year old sequence of cliffs, or just to partake of an ice cream!

Passing the top of the beach path (Wp.10 68M), we keep left, following the left fence line into the corner to pick up the obvious cliff top path, which gradually rises, mainly through scrub and light woodland, towards **Culver Down**.

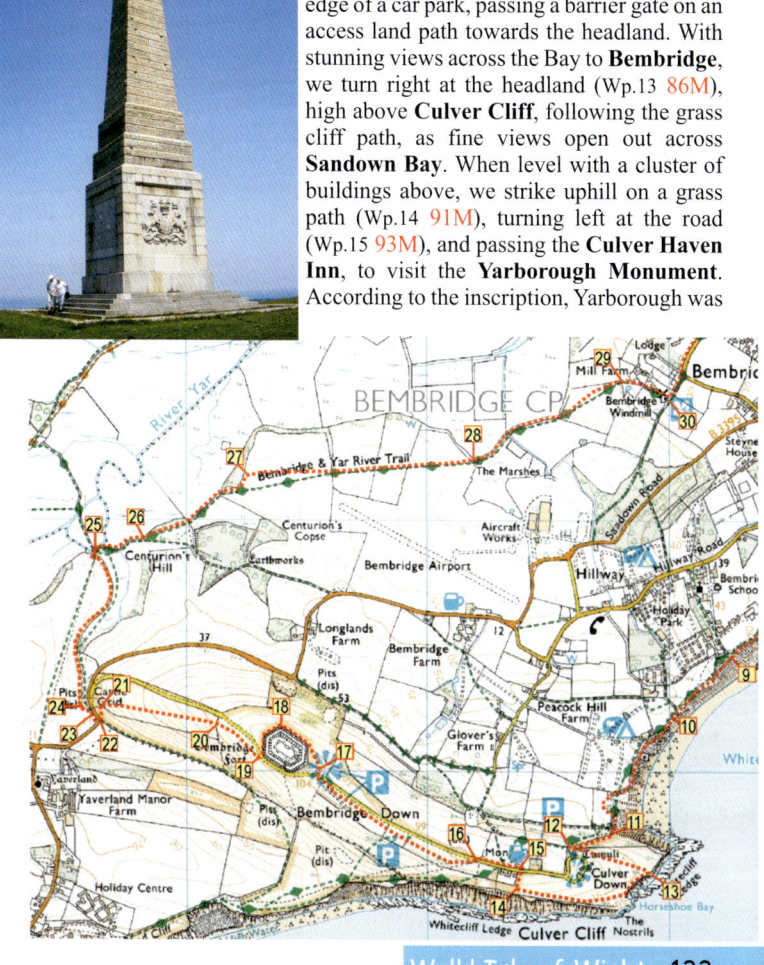

Yarborough Monument

Crossing a stile (Wp.11 78M), we emerge to go up a steep, bare, chalk downland path. We turn sharp left at the top (Wp.12 81M), around the edge of a car park, passing a barrier gate on an access land path towards the headland. With stunning views across the Bay to **Bembridge**, we turn right at the headland (Wp.13 86M), high above **Culver Cliff**, following the grass cliff path, as fine views open out across **Sandown Bay**. When level with a cluster of buildings above, we strike uphill on a grass path (Wp.14 91M), turning left at the road (Wp.15 93M), and passing the **Culver Haven Inn**, to visit the **Yarborough Monument**. According to the inscription, Yarborough was indeed an all round jolly good chap!

Regaining the road we turn right, passing a kiosk, and bearing left after a cattle grid on a grass path (Wp.16 95M), which loosely parallels the road. Going through parking and picnic areas, we cross the road by a car park entrance, just before **Bembridge Fort**, making for the octagonal viewpoint stone (Wp.17 105M) - hopefully on a clear day. We pass round the **Bembridge** side of the fort (Wp.18 109M), peering over the fence to view this impressive classic 1860's brick built fort, with goats grazing in the 'moat'.

Regaining the road, we cross, dropping down to turn right on a faint grass track (Wp.19 112M), roughly paralleling the road, before leaving the track to make for and cross a stile next to a field gate (Wp.20 115M). Making our own path down to the bottom left corner of the access land field, we pass through a field gate (Wp.21 121M), dropping down the main path to go through a kissing gate at a road (Wp.22 122M). Turning right, we soon cross the road onto a permissive footpath track (Wp.23 123M), keeping left at a fork to cross a stile next to a field gate (Wp.24 124M) and turning right along the edge of a large

field. A lovely grass path takes us along the left side of a valley bottom, eventually crossing a stile to turn right at a T-junction as we join the **Yar River Trail** (Wp.25 133M). A shady causeway path, with marshes either side, takes us to a fork by a fingerpost, where we keep left (Wp.26 136M) on BB20, turning left at a nearby fingerpost T-junction, near the edge of the woodland of **Centurion Hill**, which is thought to conceal the lost Medieval village of **Wolverton**, destroyed by the French in 1340.

Bembridge Windmill

Emerging into a meadow, we keep left up a slope, immediately bearing right (Wp.27 143M) to pass a nearby lone oak tree, and crossing the meadow along a low ridge to go over a stile. Advancing through two more fields and over a stile, we cross the end of **Bembridge** airfield runway onto BB21, a causeway path through the marshes (Wp.28 155M). After two more stiles, we climb a meadow, crossing another stile in the top left corner (Wp.29 164M) and bearing right to visit **Bembridge Windmill**. This fine mill was built around 1700, went out of use in 1913, and was restored in 1963 to be cared for by the National Trust.

Passing the mill, we turn left at a T-junction on a wide track (Wp.30 167M). Joining a road on a bend, we keep ahead, turning left at a fingerpost on footpath BB3 (Wp.31 174M), or keeping ahead for a refreshment break at **Ye Old Village Inn**. The descending woodland path bends right at the bottom onto a boardwalk (Wp.32 177M), eventually emerging on an unmade road, between houses, leading to the **Pilot Boat Inn** (Wp.33 183M). Turning left at the main road we return to the start (Wp.1 184M).

Final walk up Ryde Pier

See the notes on Using GPS on the Isle of Wight on page 16.

1

TENNYSON DOWN & THE NEEDLES

Wp	Zo	E	N
1	SZ	34533	85809
2	SZ	33939	85548
3	SZ	32491	85325
4	SZ	31885	85053
5	SZ	29970	84680
6	SZ	29903	84805
7	SZ	29634	84896
8	SZ	30790	85254
9	SZ	31600	85349
10	SZ	31525	85573
11	SZ	31354	85602
12	SZ	31543	85903
13	SZ	31265	85861
14	SZ	31895	85971
15	SZ	31930	85751
16	SZ	32400	85893
17	SZ	32478	85616
18	SZ	33280	85775
19	SZ	33590	85628
20	SZ	33898	85768
21	SZ	34088	85843
22	SZ	34375	85977

2

OLD FRESHWATER & THE FORTS

Wp	Zo	E	N
1	SZ	35316	89662
2	SZ	34705	89639
3	SZ	33820	89814
4	SZ	33783	89594
5	SZ	33219	88937
6	SZ	33565	88072
7	SZ	33715	88141
8	SZ	33805	87940
9	SZ	33946	87228
10	SZ	33945	87070
11	SZ	34113	86835
12	SZ	34241	86949
13	SZ	34323	86505
14	SZ	34455	86252
15	SZ	34553	86307
16	SZ	34660	85882
17	SZ	34680	85730
18	SZ	34943	85635
19	SZ	35015	85692
20	SZ	34940	85741
21	SZ	34990	85815
22	SZ	35346	85832
23	SZ	35110	86490
24	SZ	35087	86565
25	SZ	34672	87313
26	SZ	34740	87982
27	SZ	34755	88651
28	SZ	34758	89226
29	SZ	34770	89596

3

WESTERN YAR & YARMOUTH

Wp	Zo	E	N
1	SZ	35313	89656
2	SZ	35435	89688
3	SZ	35775	89783
4	SZ	36313	89806
5	SZ	36408	89591
6	SZ	35657	89138
7	SZ	36620	88563
8	SZ	37328	88026
9	SZ	37640	87323
10	SZ	37675	86889
11	SZ	37370	86319
12	SZ	36799	86376
13	SZ	36660	86756
14	SZ	36295	86911
15	SZ	35713	86882
16	SZ	34918	87027
17	SZ	34868	87127
18	SZ	35535	89421
19	SZ	35220	89581

4

COMPTON DOWN & FIVE BARROWS

Wp	Zo	E	N
1	SZ	34620	85732
2	SZ	34935	85640
3	SZ	35013	85697
4	SZ	35855	85740
5	SZ	37363	85677
6	SZ	39010	85191
7	SZ	39108	85089
8	SZ	39023	84991
9	SZ	38718	84869
10	SZ	38765	84561
11	SZ	38245	84604
12	SZ	38003	84182
13	SZ	37810	84147
14	SZ	37853	84107
15	SZ	37786	84093
16	SZ	37020	85052
17	SZ	36795	85212
18	SZ	36630	85402
19	SZ	36503	85434

5

HULVERSTONE TO NINGWOOD

Wp	Zo	E	N
1	SZ	39764	84019
2	SZ	40073	84534
3	SZ	40565	84303
4	SZ	40595	84509
5	SZ	40155	85044
6	SZ	39556	85076
7	SZ	39438	85041
8	SZ	38663	85289
9	SZ	38561	86054
10	SZ	38568	86391
11	SZ	38665	86894
12	SZ	39270	86778
13	SZ	39375	87258
14	SZ	39163	87308
15	SZ	39065	87950
16	SZ	39093	88120
17	SZ	38933	88563
18	SZ	39340	89352
19	SZ	39715	89857
20	SZ	39933	89480
21	SZ	40012	89178

6

THE LONG STONE

Wp	Zo	E	N
1	SZ	39760	84029
2	SZ	39668	83934
3	SZ	39225	83562
4	SZ	38978	83749
5	SZ	38892	83703
6	SZ	38005	84182
7	SZ	37805	84149
8	SZ	37855	84104
9	SZ	37785	84082
10	SZ	38575	83593
11	SZ	38633	83499
12	SZ	38693	83374
13	SZ	40905	82194
14	SZ	41308	82487
15	SZ	40665	83689
16	SZ	40563	83759
17	SZ	40495	83972
18	SZ	40720	84214
19	SZ	40053	84533

7

HAMSTEAD & THE TREE GRAVEYARD

Wp	Zo	E	N
1	SZ	39898	89176
2	SZ	40055	89182
3	SZ	39925	89480
4	SZ	40126	89929
5	SZ	40114	90384
6	SZ	41340	91037
7	SZ	41490	91215
8	SZ	40913	91980
9	SZ	40513	92000
10	SZ	39963	91320
11	SZ	39903	91157
12	SZ	39505	90873
13	SZ	39180	90888
14	SZ	39033	90679
15	SZ	38865	90675
16	SZ	37515	90120
17	SZ	37180	90065
18	SZ	37120	89743
19	SZ	36730	89898
20	SZ	35780	89806
21	SZ	35450	89718
22	SZ	35333	89653

8

SHALFLEET, WINKLE STREET & SHOREWELL

Wp	Zo	E	N
1	SZ	41417	89274
2	SZ	41363	89197
3	SZ	41503	88378
4	SZ	41445	88268
5	SZ	41355	87903
6	SZ	41309	87539
7	SZ	40990	87296
8	SZ	41210	87288
9	SZ	41198	86958
10	SZ	41493	86783
11	SZ	41833	86856
12	SZ	42505	86661
13	SZ	42435	86578
14	SZ	42191	86723
15	SZ	41750	86126
16	SZ	42340	85799
17	SZ	42380	85886
18	SZ	42580	85828
19	SZ	42925	85199
20	SZ	43083	84919
21	SZ	43268	84409
22	SZ	43123	84231
23	SZ	43793	83714
24	SZ	44620	83707
25	SZ	44978	83502
26	SZ	45458	83159
27	SZ	45448	82939
28	SZ	45654	82946

9

BRIGHSTONE & GRAMMARS COMMON

Wp	Zo	E	N
1	SZ	42818	82775
2	SZ	42720	82590
3	SZ	42405	82505
4	SZ	41547	82628
5	SZ	41305	82490
6	SZ	41315	82652
7	SZ	41418	83461
8	SZ	41615	83354
9	SZ	41635	83689
10	SZ	41268	84085
11	SZ	41275	84167
12	SZ	40720	84214
13	SZ	40565	84302
14	SZ	40593	84521
15	SZ	40218	84969
16	SZ	42075	84509
17	SZ	43420	84037
18	SZ	43550	83674
19	SZ	43318	83239
20	SZ	43010	83239

10

NEWTOWN NATURE RESERVE

Wp	Zo	E	N
1	SZ	41420	89267
2	SZ	41503	89570
3	SZ	41830	89572
4	SZ	42025	89772
5	SZ	42310	90027
6	SZ	42335	90400
7	SZ	42175	90665
8	SZ	42035	90762
9	SZ	41890	91147
10	SZ	41988	90965
11	SZ	42160	90750
12	SZ	42400	90710
13	SZ	42900	90497
14	SZ	42888	90872
15	SZ	42655	91114
16	SZ	42955	90834
17	SZ	42990	90394
18	SZ	42398	90642

11

NEWBRIDGE, SHALFLEET & CHESSELL DOWN

Wp	Zo	E	N
1	SZ	41308	87541
2	SZ	41355	87908
3	SZ	41445	88270
4	SZ	41355	89207
5	SZ	41410	89281
6	SZ	41375	89285
7	SZ	41338	89222
8	SZ	41180	89192
9	SZ	40855	88913
10	SZ	40473	88678
11	SZ	40568	88645
12	SZ	40423	87788
13	SZ	40445	87303
14	SZ	40988	87303
15	SZ	41210	87283
16	SZ	41200	86933
17	SZ	41193	86543
18	SZ	41288	86183
19	SZ	41195	86178
20	SZ	40945	85289
21	SZ	40665	85199
22	SZ	40802	85096
23	SZ	40280	85074
24	SZ	40280	85199
25	SZ	40040	85246
26	SZ	39790	85396
27	SZ	39540	85486
28	SZ	39305	85836
29	SZ	39265	86776
30	SZ	40165	86551
31	SZ	40200	86578
32	SZ	40708	87003
33	SZ	41283	87563

12

CALBOURNE & BRIGHSTONE FOREST

Wp	Zo	E	N
1	SZ	42494	86836
2	SZ	42435	86566
3	SZ	42200	86726
4	SZ	41751	86137
5	SZ	41208	86178
6	SZ	40945	85291
7	SZ	40673	85199
8	SZ	40797	85098
9	SZ	40993	84966
10	SZ	41935	84906
11	SZ	41973	84861
12	SZ	43216	84315
13	SZ	43265	84401
14	SZ	43305	84319
15	SZ	43545	84319
16	SZ	44400	04629
17	SZ	44874	84749
18	SZ	46062	85056
19	SZ	45713	85833
20	SZ	45538	85988
21	SZ	45313	85786
22	SZ	44875	86266
23	SZ	44570	86236
24	SZ	44320	85958
25	SZ	44263	86021
26	SZ	44350	87532
27	SZ	44295	87698
28	SZ	44298	88048
29	SZ	43870	87953
30	SZ	43570	87918
31	SZ	42965	87665
32	SZ	43110	87563
33	SZ	42713	87301
34	SZ	42460	87228

13

BRIGHSTONE BAY

Wp	Zo	E	N
1	SZ	42820	82774
2	SZ	43028	82669
3	SZ	43310	82352
4	SZ	43548	82277
5	SZ	43640	82130
6	SZ	44050	82012
7	SZ	44620	82070
8	SZ	44726	81974
9	SZ	44793	81840
10	SZ	45178	81732
11	SZ	45273	81420
12	SZ	45383	80973
13	SZ	45043	79969
14	SZ	44691	79850
15	SZ	44568	80230
16	SZ	43700	80790
17	SZ	42035	81795
18	SZ	42005	82060
19	SZ	42075	82437
20	SZ	42405	82502
21	SZ	42700	82609

14

GALLIBURY HUMP & BOWCOMBE DOWN

Wp	Zo	E	N
1	SZ	46490	87928
2	SZ	46678	88018
3	SZ	46643	88515
4	SZ	46210	88328
5	SZ	44860	88363
6	SZ	44643	88308
7	SZ	44238	88195
8	SZ	44348	87533
9	SZ	44258	86021
10	SZ	43953	85426
11	SZ	43812	85078
12	SZ	44767	85543
13	SZ	45547	85987
14	SZ	46100	86841
15	SZ	46885	86908
16	SZ	47052	87044
17	SZ	46810	87423

15

THORNESS BAY

Wp	Zo	E	N
1	SZ	47052	93399
2	SZ	47060	93306
3	SZ	46523	92919
4	SZ	46968	92488
5	SZ	46660	92303
6	SZ	46505	92006
7	SZ	46223	92063
8	SZ	45705	91956
9	SZ	45738	91568
10	SZ	45205	91596
11	SZ	44893	91419
12	SZ	44605	91221
13	SZ	44448	92241
14	SZ	43990	92579
15	SZ	43905	92904
16	SZ	45530	93414
17	SZ	45973	93706
18	SZ	46085	93816
19	SZ	46450	93453
20	SZ	46518	93538
21	SZ	46960	93253

16

PARKHURST FOREST

Wp	Zo	E	N
1	SZ	46505	87936
2	SZ	46673	88023
3	SZ	46645	88518
4	SZ	47578	88638
5	SZ	47623	89110
6	SZ	47423	89250
7	SZ	47334	89659
8	SZ	47300	89825
9	SZ	47365	89875
10	SZ	47630	90308
11	SZ	47725	90420
12	SZ	47325	90868
13	SZ	47283	91171
14	SZ	47245	91141
15	SZ	47051	91263
16	SZ	46788	91076
17	SZ	46614	91723
18	SZ	46498	91996
19	SZ	46228	92063
20	SZ	45703	91956
21	SZ	45805	91171
22	SZ	45075	91069
23	SZ	44780	91294
24	SZ	44624	91219
25	SZ	44813	91016
26	SZ	44645	90841
27	SZ	44585	90869
28	SZ	44540	90409
29	SZ	44512	89471
30	SZ	44480	89457
31	SZ	44469	89207
32	SZ	44586	88519
33	SZ	44844	88378
34	SZ	46210	88333
35	SZ	46401	87938

17
PORCHFIELD, GURNARD & COWES

Wp	Zo	E	N
1	SZ	44613	89497
2	SZ	44505	89472
3	SZ	44541	90409
4	SZ	44584	90874
5	SZ	44519	90874
6	SZ	44605	91215
7	SZ	45165	91774
8	SZ	45106	92496
9	SZ	45165	02544
10	SZ	45108	92639
11	SZ	45125	92888
12	SZ	45189	92898
13	SZ	45233	92950
14	SZ	45295	93121
15	SZ	45264	93328
16	SZ	45976	93700
17	SZ	46088	93813
18	SZ	47080	95383
19	SZ	47108	95331
20	SZ	47338	95506
21	SZ	47370	95431
22	SZ	47788	95565
23	SZ	47745	95718
24	SZ	47733	95888
25	SZ	49600	96387
26	SZ	49543	96357
27	SZ	49765	95777
28	SZ	50008	95626
29	SZ	50138	95566
30	SZ	50214	95664
31	SZ	50336	95568

18
SHOREWELL TO NITON

Wp	Zo	E	N
1	SZ	45652	82929
2	SZ	45374	82915
3	SZ	45320	82734
4	SZ	45180	82619
5	SZ	45524	82221
6	SZ	45600	82280
7	SZ	46070	82142
8	SZ	46079	81797
9	SZ	45999	81036
10	SZ	46351	80995
11	SZ	46270	80798
12	SZ	46503	80721
13	SZ	46748	80295
14	SZ	46664	80249
15	SZ	46744	80016
16	SZ	47278	79762
17	SZ	47903	79752
18	SZ	48038	79881
19	SZ	48349	79853
20	SZ	48481	79782
21	SZ	48516	79834
22	SZ	48565	79923
23	SZ	49259	79383
24	SZ	49613	78992
25	SZ	49589	78937
26	SZ	49560	78805
27	SZ	49573	78740
28	SZ	49680	78698
29	SZ	49500	78157
30	SZ	49612	78197
31	SZ	49689	78319
32	SZ	49768	77725
33	SZ	49843	77598
34	SZ	49985	77501
35	SZ	50010	77485
36	SZ	50599	76759
37	SZ	50735	76774
38	SZ	50725	76692

19
CHALE BAY

Wp	Zo	E	N
1	SZ	48396	77635
2	SZ	48474	77853
3	SZ	48750	77845
4	SZ	48790	77975
5	SZ	49200	78132
6	SZ	48375	78562
7	SZ	48084	78461
8	SZ	47506	78438
9	SZ	47708	78802
10	SZ	47693	78947
11	SZ	47812	79753
12	SZ	47275	79766
13	SZ	46745	80028
14	SZ	46424	80098
15	SZ	46180	80075
16	SZ	45915	80035
17	SZ	45344	79867
18	SZ	45154	79885
19	SZ	45055	79988
20	SZ	44869	79884
21	SZ	46843	78309
22	SZ	46975	78498
23	SZ	47203	78352
24	SZ	47081	78137
25	SZ	47590	77657
26	SZ	48121	77668
27	SZ	48323	77552

20
SHOREWELL & THE DOWNS

Wp	Zo	E	N
1	SZ	45643	82937
2	SZ	45813	83217
3	SZ	45858	83289
4	SZ	46504	83498
5	SZ	46651	83833
6	SZ	47393	83404
7	SZ	47451	84291
8	SZ	47492	84972
9	SZ	47223	85221
10	SZ	47142	86093
11	SZ	47121	86187
12	SZ	47365	86388
13	SZ	47894	85821
14	SZ	47693	85709
15	SZ	47860	85064
16	SZ	47849	85020
17	SZ	48333	85001
18	SZ	48543	84779
19	SZ	48530	84709
20	SZ	48645	84328
21	SZ	48279	84029
22	SZ	48029	83864
23	SZ	47757	83557
24	SZ	47590	83082
25	SZ	47690	82929
26	SZ	46648	82672
27	SZ	45841	83089
28	SZ	45818	83144

21
CARISBROOKE CASTLE & GATCOMBE

Wp	Zo	E	N
1	SZ	48626	88228
2	SZ	48554	88240
3	SZ	48530	87951
4	SZ	48445	87693
5	SZ	48299	87588
6	SZ	48228	87599
7	SZ	47571	86859
8	SZ	47616	86817
9	SZ	47280	86453
10	SZ	47360	86383
11	SZ	47121	86187
12	SZ	47135	86099
13	SZ	47218	85231
14	SZ	47495	84976
15	SZ	47864	85069
16	SZ	47844	85019
17	SZ	48328	85016
18	SZ	48551	84788
19	SZ	49235	84561
20	SZ	49155	85130
21	SZ	40574	85352
22	SZ	48616	85694
23	SZ	48645	86351
24	SZ	48740	87435
25	SZ	48655	87415
26	SZ	48588	87614
27	SZ	48789	87955
28	SZ	48724	87983
29	SZ	48613	88033

22 HOY'S MONUMENT & ST CATHERINE'S DOWN

Wp	Zo	E	N
1	SZ	50718	76774
2	SZ	50594	76757
3	SZ	50406	76919
4	SZ	50640	77388
5	SZ	50493	77440
6	SZ	50495	77585
7	SZ	50375	77820
8	SZ	50209	78115
9	SZ	50546	78407
10	SZ	50415	78702
11	SZ	49910	78768
12	SZ	49811	78969
13	SZ	49785	79170
14	SZ	49620	78983
15	SZ	49588	78925
16	SZ	49565	78793
17	SZ	49596	78803
18	SZ	49324	77777
19	SZ	49378	77292
20	SZ	49289	77227
21	SZ	49125	76739
22	SZ	48983	76647
23	SZ	49815	75969
24	SZ	50395	76157
25	SZ	50291	76604
26	SZ	50729	76694
27	SZ	51140	76369
28	SZ	50908	76559
29	SZ	50848	76639

23 NITON, GORE CLIFF & ST CATHERINE'S POINT

Wp	Zo	E	N
1	SZ	50733	76772
2	SZ	50728	76694
3	SZ	50277	76615
4	SZ	49264	76569
5	SZ	49185	76539
6	SZ	49005	76619
7	SZ	49815	75972
8	SZ	49853	75888
9	SZ	49475	75862
10	SZ	49492	75792
11	SZ	49657	75764
12	SZ	49684	75727
13	SZ	49974	75718
14	SZ	50030	75661
15	SZ	49826	75519
16	SZ	49665	75439
17	SZ	49643	75308
18	SZ	49833	75432
19	SZ	49943	75299
20	SZ	50405	75486
21	SZ	50195	75564
22	SZ	50278	75586
23	SZ	50265	75729
24	SZ	50664	75960
25	SZ	50658	76134
26	SZ	51340	76200

24 ROOKLEY AND THE CHEQUERS INN

Wp	Zo	E	N
1	SZ	50835	84112
2	SZ	50734	84199
3	SZ	50067	84017
4	SZ	49481	83752
5	SZ	49393	83889
6	SZ	49239	83884
7	SZ	48803	83032
8	SZ	48602	82851
9	SZ	48552	82639
10	SZ	48628	82130
11	SZ	49177	82244
12	SZ	49225	82357
13	SZ	49163	82449
14	SZ	49536	82619
15	SZ	49705	82440
16	SZ	50183	82763
17	SZ	50498	82568
18	SZ	50712	82485
19	SZ	51088	82698
20	SZ	51075	83016
21	SZ	50378	83263
22	SZ	50540	83378
23	SZ	50527	83823
24	SZ	50529	83931
25	SZ	50653	84151

25 RIVER MEDINA & NEWPORT

Wp	Zo	E	N
1	SZ	49965	88960
2	SZ	49981	89015
3	SZ	50018	89023
4	SZ	49993	89192
5	SZ	50105	89338
6	SZ	50200	89668
7	SZ	50335	90208
8	SZ	50888	91940
9	SZ	51103	91905
10	SZ	51578	91505
11	SZ	51670	91402
12	SZ	52405	91477
13	SZ	52398	91012
14	SZ	51770	90887
15	SZ	51593	89815
16	SZ	51320	90045
17	SZ	51235	90293
18	SZ	50939	90433
19	SZ	50360	89470
20	SZ	50235	89378
21	SZ	50158	89427

26 ST GEORGE'S DOWN & NEWPORT

Wp	Zo	E	N
1	SZ	49950	88963
2	SZ	49988	88980
3	SZ	50033	88777
4	SZ	50139	88781
5	SZ	50238	88540
6	SZ	50120	88518
7	SZ	50297	88315
8	SZ	50348	88254
9	SZ	50408	88245
10	SZ	50515	88205
11	SZ	50641	88262
12	SZ	50819	88104
13	SZ	50715	88097
14	SZ	50821	87590
15	SZ	51033	87192
16	SZ	51195	87259
17	SZ	51268	87242
18	SZ	51510	86999
19	SZ	51484	86951
20	SZ	51718	86897
21	SZ	52040	87082
22	SZ	52425	87107
23	SZ	52528	87226
24	SZ	52744	87510
25	SZ	52714	87745
26	SZ	52762	88297
27	SZ	52276	88558
28	SZ	52179	88337
29	SZ	51904	88237
30	SZ	51530	88300
31	SZ	51328	88266
32	SZ	50690	88445
33	SZ	50375	88265
34	SZ	50224	88744

27
WHITWELL, WEEK DOWN & THE UNDERCLIFF

Wp	Zo	E	N
1	SZ	52103	78064
2	SZ	52563	78382
3	SZ	52474	78667
4	SZ	52331	79013
5	SZ	52430	79045
6	SZ	52395	79125
7	SZ	52870	79080
8	SZ	52705	79265
9	SZ	52738	79650
10	SZ	53263	79800
11	SZ	53453	79603
12	SZ	53783	79108
13	SZ	53854	78909
14	SZ	53857	78621
15	SZ	54548	77232
16	SZ	54396	77192
17	SZ	54000	76979
18	SZ	53790	76917
19	SZ	53571	76804
20	SZ	53543	76867
21	SZ	53095	76549
22	SZ	52609	77107
23	SZ	52758	77139
24	SZ	52693	77184
25	SZ	52602	77299
26	SZ	52550	77770
27	SZ	52500	77867
28	SZ	52409	77865
29	SZ	52156	77932

28
APPULDURCOMBE

Wp	Zo	E	N
1	SZ	52997	81680
2	SZ	52980	81640
3	SZ	53081	81200
4	SZ	53075	81055
5	SZ	52615	80852
6	SZ	52625	80782
7	SZ	52922	80605
8	SZ	53335	80505
9	SZ	53393	80530
10	SZ	53642	79870
11	SZ	53788	79455
12	SZ	53880	79120
13	SZ	54084	79084
14	SZ	54542	79229
15	SZ	54410	79900
16	SZ	54285	80137
17	SZ	54030	80765
18	SZ	53281	81708

29
MERSLEY AND ARRETON DOWNS

Wp	Zo	E	N
1	SZ	53415	86672
2	SZ	53539	86567
3	SZ	53400	85974
4	SZ	53390	85789
5	SZ	53805	85626
6	SZ	54116	85724
7	SZ	54245	85952
8	SZ	54225	86004
9	SZ	54298	86102
10	SZ	54704	86117
11	SZ	54693	86249
12	SZ	55770	86549
13	SZ	55741	86610
14	SZ	55793	86664
15	SZ	56448	86632
16	SZ	56553	87142
17	SZ	56325	87312
18	SZ	56175	87450
19	SZ	56172	87537
20	SZ	55386	87289
21	SZ	55011	87182
22	SZ	54980	87124
23	SZ	55045	87109
24	SZ	54310	87217
25	SZ	53484	87234
26	SZ	53471	87149

30
GODSHILL TO OLD SHANKLIN

Wp	Zo	E	N
1	SZ	52996	81685
2	SZ	52979	81633
3	SZ	53090	81203
4	SZ	53021	81030
5	SZ	52845	80952
6	SZ	53392	80520
7	SZ	53325	79980
8	SZ	53440	79918
9	SZ	53444	79610
10	SZ	53793	79463
11	SZ	53636	79873
12	SZ	53655	80247
13	SZ	53793	80520
14	SZ	54303	81050
15	SZ	54650	81178
16	SZ	55050	81113
17	SZ	55630	80722
18	SZ	55840	80650
19	SZ	56189	80312
20	SZ	56643	80212
21	SZ	56735	80109
22	SZ	57085	80500
23	SZ	57823	80522
24	SZ	58089	80772
25	SZ	58161	81113

31
WOOTON OLD MILL POND & HAVENSTREET

Wp	Zo	E	N
1	SZ	54665	91971
2	SZ	54630	91974
3	SZ	54533	91836
4	SZ	54405	91506
5	SZ	54645	91494
6	SZ	54470	91299
7	SZ	54330	90869
8	SZ	54400	90544
9	SZ	54315	90049
10	SZ	54743	89970
11	SZ	54975	89615
12	SZ	54960	89530
13	SZ	54899	89475
14	SZ	54528	89408
15	SZ	54548	88850
16	SZ	54368	88735
17	SZ	53979	88457
18	SZ	53908	88372
19	SZ	54235	88095
20	SZ	54349	87982
21	SZ	54245	87882
22	SZ	54914	87871
23	SZ	55347	87937
24	SZ	55895	87937
25	SZ	56361	88115
26	SZ	56563	88110
27	SZ	57105	89110
28	SZ	57340	89329
29	SZ	57088	89364
30	SZ	56511	89802
31	SZ	56532	89965
32	SZ	56192	90304
33	SZ	55960	90259
34	SZ	56020	90344
35	SZ	55958	90704
36	SZ	55768	91029
37	SZ	55665	90684
38	SZ	55145	90861
39	SZ	55243	91074
40	SZ	55085	91374
41	SZ	55095	91434
42	SZ	55315	91623
43	SZ	54963	92008

32
THE WHITE WELL, ST LAWRENCE, ...AH
VENTNOR & LUCCOMBE

Wp	Zo	E	N
1	SZ	52211	77780
2	SZ	52229	77717
3	SZ	52405	77877
4	SZ	52508	77870
5	SZ	52554	77767
6	SZ	52609	77304
7	SZ	52741	77182
8	SZ	52625	77118
9	SZ	53095	76547
10	SZ	53190	76509
11	SZ	53173	76407
12	SZ	53261	76414
13	SZ	53075	76327
14	SZ	53218	76269
15	SZ	53316	76142
16	SZ	53448	76254
17	SZ	53520	76159
18	SZ	54523	76684
19	SZ	54575	76794
20	SZ	54941	76892
21	SZ	55013	76893
22	SZ	55939	77302
23	SZ	56303	77357
24	SZ	57795	77902
25	SZ	57803	78035
26	SZ	58161	78517
27	SZ	58233	78940
28	SZ	58087	79350
29	SZ	58035	79365
30	SZ	57768	79385
31	SZ	57850	79668
32	SZ	57765	79802

33
WROXALL HORSESHOE & AMERICA WOOD

Wp	Zo	E	N
1	SZ	55123	79665
2	SZ	55343	79025
3	SZ	55669	78457
4	SZ	56998	78684
5	SZ	57265	78975
6	SZ	57042	79643
7	SZ	56744	80122
8	SZ	56605	80530
9	SZ	56579	80684
10	SZ	56741	81206
11	SZ	56721	81449
12	SZ	56804	82060
13	SZ	56738	82043
14	SZ	56708	82023
15	SZ	56390	82084
16	SZ	56303	81955
17	SZ	55789	82110
18	SZ	55752	81482
19	SZ	55836	80642
20	SZ	56008	80524
21	SZ	55585	80320
22	SZ	55063	79925

34
QUARR ABBEY

Wp	Zo	E	N
1	SZ	54664	91979
2	SZ	54965	92013
3	SZ	55328	91638
4	SZ	55913	91508
5	SZ	55854	91238
6	SZ	56093	91163
7	SZ	56136	91341
8	SZ	56248	91263
9	SZ	56005	90908
10	SZ	56382	90712
11	SZ	56625	91498
12	SZ	56748	91683
13	SZ	56565	92160
14	SZ	56415	92295
15	SZ	56540	92615
16	SZ	56299	92539
17	SZ	56228	92702
18	SZ	56105	92583
19	SZ	55715	92618
20	SZ	55478	92618
21	SZ	55403	92656
22	SZ	55187	92175

35
SANDOWN TO ARRETON

Wp	Zo	E	N
1	SZ	59387	83810
2	SZ	59394	83896
3	SZ	59225	83873
4	SZ	59101	84036
5	SZ	59260	84404
6	SZ	59206	84416
7	SZ	58843	84996
8	SZ	58799	85131
9	SZ	57768	85579
10	SZ	57398	85817
11	SZ	57230	85764
12	SZ	56891	85489
13	SZ	56903	85631
14	SZ	56735	85686
15	SZ	56438	85654
16	SZ	56175	85624
17	SZ	55960	85888
18	SZ	54370	85441
19	SZ	54358	85496
20	SZ	54033	85511
21	SZ	53390	85789
22	SZ	53400	85974
23	SZ	53545	86549
24	SZ	53410	86669

36
BONCHURCH CHALLENGE & THE DEVIL'S CHIMNEY

Wp	Zo	E	N
1	SZ	57795	78397
2	SZ	57670	78162
3	SZ	57603	78089
4	SZ	57267	78030
5	SZ	57515	78195
6	SZ	57492	78267
7	SZ	57438	78242
8	SZ	57418	78300
9	SZ	57359	78610
10	SZ	56988	78685
11	SZ	56334	78477
12	SZ	56153	78687
13	SZ	55874	79231
14	SZ	56673	79800
15	SZ	56963	79758
16	SZ	57266	78895
17	SZ	57356	78688
18	SZ	58023	78910
19	SZ	58118	78852
20	SZ	58049	78680
21	SZ	58146	78594
22	SZ	57961	78055
23	SZ	57822	77983
24	SZ	57675	78080

37
NEWCHURCH & ASHEY DOWN

Wp	Zo	E	N
1	SZ	56154	85469
2	SZ	56178	85629
3	SZ	56438	85644
4	SZ	56733	85686
5	SZ	56905	85639
6	SZ	57399	85819
7	SZ	57220	85917
8	SZ	57483	86429
9	SZ	57680	87292
10	SZ	57603	87346
11	SZ	58224	87927
12	SZ	58143	88360
13	SZ	58170	88397
14	SZ	57702	88852
15	SZ	57490	87947
16	SZ	57424	87907
17	SZ	57448	87567
18	SZ	57150	87550
19	SZ	57135	87414
20	SZ	56589	87151
21	SZ	56608	86897
22	SZ	57000	86672
23	SZ	57048	86549
24	SZ	56450	86334
25	SZ	56457	85978
26	SZ	55953	85904
27	SZ	56060	85754

38
BRADING DOWN & BLOODSTONE COPSE

Wp	Zo	E	N
1	SZ	60575	87070
2	SZ	60635	87320
3	SZ	60618	87254
4	SZ	60220	87460
5	SZ	60145	87578
6	SZ	59780	87705
7	SZ	59179	87852
8	SZ	58693	87965
9	SZ	58535	87965
10	SZ	58300	87810
11	SZ	57981	87262
12	SZ	59095	86997
13	SZ	60085	86742
14	SZ	60133	86784
15	SZ	60255	86787
16	SZ	60309	86857
17	SZ	60493	86824
18	SZ	60523	86924
19	SZ	60572	86926

39
ST HELENS & PRIORY BAY

Wp	Zo	E	N
1	SZ	62568	89000
2	SZ	62454	89195
3	SZ	62180	89275
4	SZ	62145	89679
5	SZ	61895	89794
6	SZ	61885	90079
7	SZ	62654	90005
8	SZ	62896	89993
9	SZ	63055	90293
10	SZ	63198	90866
11	SZ	63391	90706
12	SZ	63473	90303
13	SZ	63700	89490
14	SZ	63723	89315
15	SZ	63680	88887
16	SZ	63480	89020
17	SZ	63138	88715
18	SZ	63001	89081
19	SZ	62825	89070

40
BEMBRIDGE & CULVER DOWN

Wp	Zo	E	N
1	SZ	64218	88660
2	SZ	64055	88785
3	SZ	64108	8887 0
4	SZ	65638	88087
5	SZ	65695	87420
6	SZ	65468	87254
7	SZ	65457	87295
8	SZ	64714	86912
9	SZ	64251	86469
10	SZ	64010	86232
11	SZ	63758	85756
12	SZ	63583	85700
13	SZ	63924	85629
14	SZ	63363	85531
15	SZ	63378	85606
16	SZ	63210	85649
17	SZ	62558	86014
18	SZ	62393	86177
19	SZ	62292	86059
20	SZ	62125	86187
21	SZ	61644	86264
22	SZ	61633	86197
23	SZ	61610	86232
24	SZ	61570	86264
25	SZ	61629	86878
26	SZ	61823	86922
27	SZ	62245	87184
28	SZ	63194	87243
29	SZ	63805	87565
30	SZ	64004	87475
31	SZ	64303	88062
32	SZ	64110	88182
33	SZ	64273	88655

Pubs, Inns, Tea Rooms and Cafes.

Isle of Wight local dialing code is 01983 if calling from the mainland.
Albion Hotel, Freshwater Bay (755755); Anchor Inn, West Cowes (292823);
Bargeman's Rest, Newport (525828); Blacksmiths Arms, Calbourne Road
(529263); Bonchurch Inn, Bonchurch (852611); Brighstone Tea Rooms
(740370); Buddle Inn, Niton Undercliffe (730243);
Bugle Inn, Brading (407359); Bugle Inn, Yarmouth (760272);
Chequers Inn, Rookley (840314); Crown Inn, Shorewell (740293);
Eight Bells, Carisbrooke (825501); Fat Cat Bar, Freshwater Bay (758500);
Fishbourne Inn, Fishbourne (882823); Four Seasons Inn, Wroxall (854701)
Gatcombe Farm Tea Gardens (721580); George Hotel, Yarmouth (760331)
Griffin, Godshill (840039); Highdown Inn (752450);
Horse and Groom, Ningwood (760672); Medina Quay, Newport (825082);
New Inn, Shalfleet (531314); Pointer Inn, Newchurch (865202);
Priory Bay Hotel (613146); Quay Arts centre, Newport (822490);
Red Lion Inn, Old Freshwater (754925); Ship and Castle, East Cowes
(280967); Sloop Inn, Wooton Bridge (882544);
Smugglers Haven Tea Gardens, Bonchurch (852992);
Snooty Fox, Brading (404021); Sportsman's Rest, Porchfield (522044);
Spyglass Inn, Ventnor (855338); Sun Inn, Calbourne (531231);
Sun Inn, Hulverstone (741124); Three Bishops, Brighstone (740226);
Village Inn, Shanklin (862514); Vine Inn, St Helens (472416);
Warren Farm Farmhouse Cream Teas (753200);
Waverly, Carisbrooke (522338); Wheatsheaf, Brading (407325);
White Hart, Havenstreet (883485); White Horse, Whitwell (730375);
White Lion, Arreton (528479); White Lion, Niton (730293);
Wight Mouse Inn, Chale (730731); Worsley, Wroxall (853144).

Useful Web Sites

Access Land www.countrysideaccess.gov.uk
Admiralty Tide Times www.easytide.com
BBC Weather www.bbc.co.uk/weather
Birding on the Isle of Wight www.dbhale.members.beeb.net
Buses, Trains and Ferries on the Isle of Wight www.iow.tbctimes.com
Discovery Walking Guides www.walking.demon.co.uk
Hampshire and Isle of Wight Wildlife trust www.hwt.org.uk
Hovertravel Passenger Ferry www.hovertravel.co.uk
Island Line Railway www.islandline.co.uk
Isle of Wight Branch of Camra www.wightwash.org.uk
Isle of Wight Index (lots of general information) www.wightindex.com
Isle of Wight Natural History Society www.iwnhas.org
Isle of Wight Rights of Way www.iwight.com/rightsofwaymaps
Isle of Wight Steam Railway www.iwsteamrailway.co.uk
Isle of Wight Walking Festival www.isleofwightwalkingfestival.co.uk
Lots of excellent general Isle of Wight information www.invectis.co.uk/iow
Met Office Weather www.metoffice.gov.uk
Naturally Wight www.wightonline.co.uk/wight/index.html
Official Site of Isle of Wight Tourism www.islandbreaks.co.uk
Quarr Abbey www.quarrabbey.co.uk Red Funnel Ferries www.redfunnel.co.uk
Southern Vectis Buses www.islandbuses.info
Stagecoach Buses www.stagecoachbus.com/south
UK Butterfly Identification www.ukbutterflies.co.uk
UK Fossils, Isle of Wight www.ukfossils.co.uk/iow.htm
Wightlink Ferries www.wightlink.co.uk
Youth Hostels Association www.yha.org.uk